Eschatology, Liturgy, and Christology

them "continuity in the communion of saints, prayers for or about the dead, the meaning of death, purgation, an interim state between death and the final general judgment, and the promise of resurrection."[20] At the end, both sides agreed that "prayer for the dead, considered within the framework of the communion of saints, need not be a church-dividing or communion-hindering issue for Lutherans and Catholics."[21] The book is a treasure trove of patristic texts, ecclesial documents, and theological writings on the subject of eschatology.

Outline

In chapter 1 we will look at the loss of the eschatological imagination, illustrating it with examples from the liturgy. We will also consider certain developments in contemporary theology touching on Christology, ecclesiology, and the mission of the church in the light of religious pluralism that bear on the question of eschatology. We will introduce three themes closely related to eschatology: creation, time, and memory.

Chapter 2 will consider the Israelite experience of God as a God in relationship to a people, a God of the covenant who remembers, and the emergence of the hope that this God, the God of the living, might also be a God who delivers the dead from Sheol and raises them to life. This will introduce the biblical categories of eschatology and apocalyptic.

Chapter 3 will seek to unpack the Johannine description of Jesus as "the way and the truth and the life" (John 14:6). It will involve considering Jesus' proclamation of the kingdom of God, the concept of discipleship, the paschal mystery, and what medieval theology called the imitation of Christ (*imitatio Christi*). We will also consider the emergence of modern individualism and how the kingdom of God is understood by a number of contemporary theologians.

Chapter 4 will move from the mystery of the resurrection to an exploration of what we might understand by the risen body. We will consider Paul's language about a "spiritual body," the different ways the risen body was imagined in the Middle Ages, and how we might ground our eschatological hope today. We will look at the social nature of the resurrection and the apocalyptic imagination.

---

20. U.S. Lutheran–Roman Catholic Dialogue, "The Hope of Eternal Life" (2010), preface.

21. Ibid., 71; the Lutheran Church–Missouri Synod stated that more work remained to be done before the remaining differences could no longer constitute an obstacle to communion (ibid., 315n).

Ratzinger's *Eschatology* is one of his best, most systematic works.[14] Ratzinger's strength is his vast knowledge of Scripture and the Christian tradition, both philosophical and theological. His emphasis on the need for an "eschatological realism" should be taken seriously.[15] Dermot Lane's *Keeping Hope Alive* is also a very fine, comprehensive work.[16] Lane engages a broad spectrum of contemporary authors and theologies; he is concerned to reclaim an eschatological vision in a culture that would rather ignore death and dying, and he also wants to reclaim an apocalyptic eschatology with its social dimensions. Significantly, he also emphasizes the connection between eschatology and liturgy. Brian Robinette's *Grammars of Resurrection* focuses on the resurrection as the "grammar" of the New Testament; once grasped in faith, it opens up the believer to the eschatological "irruption" into our world.[17] He also deals with how retrieving an apocalyptic imagination can be transformative, touching on issues of embodiment, justice, violence, and forgiveness.

Terence Nichols's approach in his book *Death and Afterlife* is more apologetic; he seeks to respond to scientific and naturalistic challenges to resurrection faith.[18] He considers the phenomenon of "near-death" experiences as one stream of evidence suggesting that the soul or mind can survive physical death, while his exploration of resurrection and eschatology introduces the theme of hope. Finally, Bruce Morrill's *Anamnesis as Dangerous Memory* is very helpful in relating eschatology and liturgy. It is also a fine introduction to the work of Johann Baptist Metz.[19]

As I was finishing this work, the common statement of Round XI of the U.S. Lutheran–Roman Catholic Dialogue appeared, entitled "The Hope of Eternal Life." Much of this common statement was taken up with contentious issues from the debates of the sixteenth century, among

14. Joseph Ratzinger, *Eschatology: Death and Eternal Life*, 2nd ed., trans. Michael Waldstein (Washington, DC: Catholic University of America Press, 1988), 8; first published in German in 1977.

15. Pope Benedict XVI, *Light of the World: The Pope, the Church, and the Signs of the Times; A Conversation with Peter Seewald* (San Francisco: Ignatius, 2010), 180.

16. Dermont A. Lane, *Keeping Hope Alive: Stirrings in Christian Theology* (New York: Paulist, 1996).

17. Brian D. Robinette, *Grammars of Resurrection: A Christian Theology of Presence and Absence* (New York: Crossroad, 2009), 23.

18. Terence Nichols, *Death and Afterlife: A Theological Introduction* (Grand Rapids, MI: Brazos, 2010).

19. Bruce T. Morrill, *Anamnesis as Dangerous Memory: Political and Liturgical Theology in Dialogue* (Collegeville, MN: Liturgical Press, 2000).

it, *pace* Joseph Ratzinger / Pope Benedict XVI, and can salvation, symbolized by the kingdom of God, be so easily separated from the person of Jesus the Christ, as Roger Haight and others suggest? How should we understand the resurrection of the body and a related concept, the immortality of the soul? Can the soul exist without the body? What is the relation between eschatology and creation? Can we say that Jesus is the cause of salvation? And can the mission of the church be reduced to witnessing to the kingdom of God without abandoning the Christian confession that Jesus is the way, the truth, and the life (cf. John 14:6)? We will explore some of these questions in this book.

Taking our point of departure from the testimony of the Scriptures and the faith of the church, we will rely on contemporary authors to help us imagine and better understand the mystery of God's future, disclosed or suggested by the story of Jesus and his preaching of the kingdom of God. Methodologically, our approach could be described as "postcritical," after the example of Avery Dulles.[12] We will attempt to navigate between a rationalism that limits knowledge to what science or a postmodern mentality finds acceptable and a biblical literalism that confuses the symbol with the intelligibility it seeks to express.

Finally, I want to call attention to an observation made by Russian Orthodox theologian Sergius Bulgakov. He points out that apart from the Nicene Creed's confession of belief in Christ's coming again in glory to judge the living and the dead, the resurrection of the body, and the life of the world to come, eschatological theology remains open to inquiry. Cautioning against the Roman Catholic tendency toward what he calls a dogmatic maximalism, he reminds us that "there are mysteries of the future age, unfathomable destinies and untraceable paths of God (Rom 11:33), that are perhaps not destined to be fully revealed in this age."[13] With this caution in mind, we will explore the images, symbols, and concepts used in the Christian tradition to convey the fullness of our salvation.

Interlocutors

Several recent works on eschatology have been most helpful in preparing this book. Their authors will be our principal interlocutors. Joseph

---

12. See Patrick W. Carey, "Cardinal Avery Dulles, S.J., among the Theologians: A Memorial Reflection," *Theological Studies* 71 (2010): 775–78.

13. Sergius Bulgakov, *The Bride of the Lamb*, trans. Boris Jakim (Grand Rapids, MI: William B. Eerdmans, 2002) 380–82 at 382.

on the biblical idea of the resurrection of the body and all its implications. Even many Christians think of the resurrection solely in personal terms. Salvation has been understood individualistically; we speak of "saving my soul," "going to heaven," or "being saved."

Too often in our Western culture the hoped-for *eschaton* has been replaced by an almost exclusive emphasis on the *eschata*, the "four last things" each of us must one day face—death and judgment, heaven and hell. But eschatology cannot be reduced to the salvation of the individual or limited to the saved. Many have lost sight of what James Alison calls "the fullness of the density of the resurrection,"[9] a wonderful way of suggesting how much is embraced by the mystery of our salvation, the proper object of the study of eschatology. They do not see how the earth itself might be included in God's salvation. Jürgen Moltmann says that "if Christian hope is reduced to the salvation of the soul in a heaven beyond death, it loses its power to renew life and change the world, and its flame is quenched."[10]

Karl Rahner argues that individual eschatology can be complete only if a collective eschatology is developed, one that includes the world and its history.[11] For the early Christians, God's future was a radically social reality; God's salvation was revealed in the resurrection of Jesus and already present initially in the gathering (*ekklesia*, "church") of the saints, particularly in their worship. It meant the age of salvation, gathering all the elect into the new creation, had already begun. The expectant faith of the early Christians was evident especially when they celebrated the Eucharist, what Paul calls in 1 Corinthians 11:20 "the Lord's supper," proclaiming the final coming of the crucified Jesus, now raised and made Lord: "For as often as you eat this bread and drink the cup, you proclaim the death of the Lord until he comes" (1 Cor 11:26).

Thus, one cannot write about eschatology without also addressing issues involving Christology, soteriology, the mission of the church, and the liturgy. We will have to consider what eschatology suggests about our salvation, both now and in the world to come. In what sense can we say that salvation is already present within history rather than beyond

9. James Alison, *Raising Abel: The Recovery of the Eschatological Imagination* (New York: Crossroad, 1996), 28.

10. Jürgen Moltmann, *The Coming of God: Christian Eschatology* (Minneapolis: Fortress, 1996), xv.

11. See Karl Rahner, *Foundations of Christian Faith* (New York: Seabury, 1978), 444–45.

Chapter 5 will investigate the *eschaton* and the *eschata*. It will begin with the more philosophical concept of the soul, rooted in the late Old Testament and Greek thought and long used in Christian tradition and the popular imagination to express faith in life beyond the grave. From there it will move to consider the *eschata*, popular symbols such as heaven, hell, judgment, the second coming, and purgatory, in the effort to grasp their fundamental intelligibility. Finally, it will address the difficult question of the *eschaton*, a corporate eschatology symbolized by the victory of justice and "a new heaven and a new earth."

Chapter 6 will return to the relation between eschatology and liturgy. It will look at the relation between liturgical time and memory and will critique some aspects of contemporary liturgical piety and practice. It will also consider the relation between liturgy and social justice and suggest ways to retrieve the eschatological imagination, so prominent in the liturgical experience of the early Christians.

Chapter 7 will offer some concluding reflections. First, it will return to the relationship between image and meaning, raised in this introduction. Then it will try to draw together some of the questions in Christology, soteriology, and ecclesiology running through this book in a way that is both appreciative and critical of contemporary theological works. It will ask whether eschatology and the doctrine of salvation can be separated from the person of Jesus and how the mission of the church should be addressed in the situation of religious pluralism.

Eschatology, Liturgy, and Christology

Toward Recovering an Eschatological Imagination

Thomas P. Rausch, SJ

A Michael Glazier Book

LITURGICAL PRESS
Collegeville, Minnesota

www.litpress.org

A Michael Glazier Book published by Liturgical PressCover design by Ann Blattner. *The Last Judgment* by Fra Angelico, ca. 1400–1455.

1   2   3   4   5   6   7   8

Library of Congress Cataloging-in-Publication Data

Rausch, Thomas P.
    Eschatology, liturgy, and christology : toward recovering an eschatological imagination / Thomas P. Rausch.
        p.   cm.
    "A Michael Glazier book."
    Includes bibliographical references and index.
    ISBN 978-0-8146-5735-5 — ISBN 978-0-8146-8051-3 (e-book)
    1. Hope—Religious aspects—Catholic Church.   2. Eschatology.
3. Imagination—Religious aspects—Catholic Church.   4. Catholic Church—Doctrines.   I. Title.

BV4638.R38   2012
236—dc23   2011051285

For

John D. McAnulty, SJ

In Memoriam

Contents

Acknowledgments

I would like to acknowledge those who have been of help in preparing this manuscript. Hans Christoffersen, editorial director at Liturgical Press, first suggested that I do a book on eschatology. Bruce Morrill was most helpful with suggestions when I was preparing a course on liturgy and ecclesiology that provided some of the background. Michael Downey, a friend and colleague of many years, read and critiqued the manuscript. Eric Christensen did the copyediting with great care. My research assistant Melanie Nguyen was a great help in checking the page proofs.

A number of friends and colleagues reviewed particular chapters or offered suggestions, among them Christopher Chapple, John Baldovin, James Fredericks, and Saba Soomekh. For their help I am grateful. The interpretation remains my own.

For occasional lapses from the use of inclusive language in speaking of God, especially in citing other authors or texts, I ask the reader's indulgence.

Thomas P. Rausch, SJ

Abbreviations

Documents of the Second Vatican Council

GS   *Gaudium et Spes* (Pastoral Constitution on the Church in the
      Modern World)
LG   *Lumen Gentium* (Dogmatic Constitution on the Church)
SC   *Sacrosanctum Concilium* (Constitution on the Sacred Liturgy)

Other

CDF   Congregation for the Doctrine of the Faith
DS   Denzinger-Schönmetzer, *Enchiridion Symbolorum*, 33rd ed.
      (Freiburg: Herder, 1965)
FABC Federation of Asian Bishops' Conferences

Introduction

What is our hope as Christians? To what do we look forward? Does God forget the countless victims of history? What about our beloved dead? What future does God have in store for us? Will it involve our beautiful earth? To raise these questions is to ask about eschatology, the end times, from the Greek *eschatos*, the "last" or "end." We look forward to the *eschaton*, the coming of the age of salvation.

Eschatology should occupy a central place in our Christian faith; without it we have no hope. In Karl Barth's words, "if Christianity be not altogether thoroughgoing eschatology, there remains in it no relationship whatever with Christ."[1] A library catalogue search reveals multitudinous volumes dealing with eschatology. Many, written from a conservative evangelical perspective, speculate about the second coming of Christ, resulting in a proliferation of millennial theologies—premillennial, amillennial, postmillennial—rooted in Revelation 20, which anticipates a thousand-year period in which Satan will be confined in the abyss and the saved will reign with Christ.[2] Fundamentalists like Tim LaHaye and Jerry Jenkins, authors of the popular *Left Behind* series, imagine the Rapture when Christ returns to take up the "saved" before the Tribulation (cf. 1 Thess 4:17), with Catholics among those left behind.[3]

On the theological left, eschatology is too often reduced to an empowering symbol or a utopian vision of justice and peace in this world. Those

---

1. Karl Barth, *The Epistle to the Romans* (London: Oxford University Press, 1933), 314.

2. See Hans Schwarz, *Eschatology* (Grand Rapids, MI: William B. Eerdmans, 2000), 322–37.

3. See Carl E. Olson, *Will Catholics Be "Left Behind"? A Catholic Critique of the Rapture and Today's Prophecy Preachers* (San Francisco: Ignatius, 2003).

in the late Robert Funk's Jesus Seminar have tried to promote the idea of a noneschatological Jesus.[4] Others doing theology today in the new context of religious pluralism have challenged traditional positions in the areas of Christology, soteriology, and the mission of the church. While much of their work has been fruitful for theology, at the same time there are methodological turns or conclusions that have significant implications for Christian eschatology and raise some troubling questions. Some are hesitant to affirm Jesus' divinity or his role in bringing the *eschaton*. He becomes one of a number of mediators of salvation, not the one who accomplishes our salvation. The church's mission becomes one of witnessing to the kingdom of God.[5] Others like John Polkinghorne, theoretical physicist and Anglican priest, focus on eschatology in an effort to bring science and religion together.[6]

In systematic theology, eschatology does not always get the attention it deserves. Dermot Lane calls it "the missing link in much contemporary theology."[7] Still less have those theologians who do stress eschatology been concerned with its relation to the Eucharist; nor have liturgists always been attentive to this relationship, as a review of the indexes of many books on liturgy indicates. Among those theologians and liturgists attentive to the eschatological dimensions of the Eucharist, I would include Dermot Lane, Johann Baptist Metz, Bruce Morrill, John Reumann, Don Saliers, Geoffrey Wainwright, and Joseph Ratzinger, now Pope Benedict XVI. We will draw on their works.

At the heart of Christian eschatology is the idea of the resurrection of the dead, based on the resurrection of Jesus. The 2006 Faith Matters survey found that 70 percent of Americans believe in the afterlife,[8] but for many of them, their idea of life beyond death is vague and undefined, more of a cultural idea about spiritual survival than something based

---

4. See, for example, Marcus J. Borg, *Jesus in Contemporary Scholarship* (Valley Forge, PA: Trinity Press International, 1994), 7–8.

5. Some of these are explored as early as 1976 in J. Peter Schineller, "Christ and Church: A Spectrum of Views," *Theological Studies* 37/4 (1976): 545–66.

6. John C. Polkinghorne, *The God of Hope and the End of the World* (New Haven, CT: Yale University Press, 2002).

7. Dermot A. Lane, *Keeping Hope Alive: Stirrings in Christian Theology* (New York: Paulist, 1996), 5; for a survey of eschatology in twentieth-century theology, see Schwartz, *Eschatology*, 107–72.

8. Robert D. Putnam and David E. Campbell, *American Grace* (New York: Simon and Schuster, 2010), 71.

1

The Eschatological Imagination

When the early Christians celebrated the Eucharist, their eschatological imagination was much in evidence. Their faith was understood communally. They saw themselves as "the saints" or "holy ones," the community of the redeemed, sharing in the divine life of Father, Son, and Holy Spirit. They gathered on Sunday, the first day of the week, to commemorate the resurrection of Jesus. The Eucharist itself symbolized the great messianic banquet in the kingdom, and their liturgies expressed in prayer and posture their hope for the Lord's Parousia or Second Coming. The church at Corinth proclaimed the Lord's death "until he comes" (1 Cor 11:26). The *Didache* offers a eucharistic prayer with strong eschatological overtones, praying that the church "be brought together from the ends of the earth" into the kingdom God has prepared (*Didache* 9:4; 10:5).[1] Their liturgical texts included the Aramaic prayer *Maranatha* (1 Cor 16:22; Rev 22:20; *Didache* 10:6) for Christ's coming. Not easily translated, *Maranatha* can mean both a petition, "Come, Lord Jesus," and also the statement that indeed "the Lord has come." Most scholars today see it as having both a present and a future reference; the congregation proclaims that the Lord has come in the Eucharist and will come again.[2]

---

1. Brian E. Daley, *The Hope of the Early Church: A Handbook of Patristic Eschatology* (Cambridge: Cambridge University Press, 1991), 12.

2. Geoffrey Wainwright, *Eucharist and Eschatology* (New York: Oxford University Press, 1981), 69–70; Joseph Ratzinger, *Eschatology: Death and Eternal Life*, 2nd ed., trans. Michael Waldstein (Washington, DC: Catholic University of America Press, 1988), 6–7.

As they gathered for liturgy, these early Christians prayed facing east toward the rising sun, the symbol of the risen Christ, now reigning and who would return to establish the kingdom of God in the world.[3] The Syrian document called *The Teaching of the Apostles* or sometimes the *Canons of the Apostles* included the following instruction:

> Pray ye towards the east: because, "as the lightning which lighteneth from the east and is seen even to the west, so shall the coming of the Son of man be"—that by this we might know and understand that He will appear from the east suddenly.[4]

The Lord's Prayer, included in these early gatherings of the church, also includes a present and future reference. Those assembled prayed for the coming of the kingdom and expressed their belief that the great feast of the end times had already begun in their Eucharist. Gordon Lathrop says that the prayer "breathes a sense of eschatology," filled with petitions for the coming Day of God together with some fears for the terrors expected in the last times; but there are "also two strong indications that the expected, longed-for Day has already dawned in the life of the community itself" in the petition about the "bread of the feast before your face."[5] Thus the assembly celebrated Christ's presence sacramentally and looked forward to his triumphant return to judge the living and the dead and to establish the kingdom in its fullness.

Fairly early, in both the Western church and the classical Eastern liturgies, with the exception of the Egyptian tradition, *Maranatha* was replaced by the phrase "blessed is he who comes in the name of the Lord," following the *Sanctus*. An ambiguous phrase, Geoffrey Wainwright suggests that it referred to "the present coming of the one who has come and who is still to come" and was thus a suitable replacement of *Maranatha*.[6]

Wainwright gives numerous examples of how the classical liturgies of both East and West saw the eucharistic meal as sign, pledge, and anticipation of the meal of the eternal kingdom to come.

---

3. Ratzinger, *Eschatology*, 6–8.

4. *Syrian Documents Attributed to the First Three Centuries*, trans. B. P. Pratten (Edinburgh: T. & T. Clark, 1871) 38, in *Ante-Nicene Christian Library*, vol. XX, ed. Alexander Roberts and James Donaldson, (Edinburgh: T. & T. Clark, 1871).

5. Gordon W. Lathrop, *Holy People: A Liturgical Ecclesiology* (Minneapolis: Fortress Press, 2006), 33–34.

6. Wainwright, *Eucharist and Eschatology*, 71–72; first attested by Caesarius of Arles (d. 542), note 223.

One frequent and simple way of expressing the relation, especially in the West, is to attach the epithet "heavenly" to various items or aspects of the eucharistic celebration. The eucharistic table is the heavenly table (*mensa caelestis*) at which is enjoyed the heavenly banquet (*convivium caeleste*) of the heavenly gifts (*dona caelestia*) of the heavenly bread (*panis caelestis*) and the heavenly cup (*poculum caeleste*), the whole being a heavenly mystery (*mysterium caeleste*). In some Eastern traditions the eucharistic table is called the royal table, which suggests both the king and his kingdom.[7]

Wainwright also gives numerous examples of liturgies that mention Christ's return or "second advent" and final judgment at the end of the institution narrative and in the anamnesis, most of them from the East. In the Greek tradition, the bringing forward of the gifts to the altar by the deacons at the Great Entry, dating from the sixth century, was greeted by the celebrant with "Blessed is he that cometh in the name of the Lord," preparing for the response "Let us stand in prayer before the holy table of God and find the grace of mercy in the day of his appearing and at the second coming our Lord and Savior Jesus Christ." The anamnesis of the Mozarabic liturgy, the Byzantine liturgies of St. Basil and St. John Chrysostom, and the Armenian liturgy all mention in various forms the Second Coming. The Syrian liturgy of Addai and Mari, the Maronite liturgy, and the liturgies of St. Basil and St. John Chrysostom pray for pardon on the Day of Judgment.

The *Sursum corda*, the call to "Lift up your hearts" occurring in the opening dialogue of all classical eucharistic prayers, Wainwright suggests is a call to prepare to meet the Lord coming either in the cult itself or eschatologically. Theodore of Mopsuestia (350–428) connected the Eucharist with the coming of Christ to raise the dead, represented symbolically. John of Damascus (676–749) explained the reasons for facing east during worship to include expectation of Christ's return from the east. The Eastern churches especially looked forward liturgically to Christ's return. However, Wainwright notes that in the eucharistic texts in the West, there is practically never any reference to the second coming of Christ. Instead, more emphasis was placed on the remission of sins through the offering of the sacrifice.[8]

7. Wainwright, *Eucharist and Eschatology*, 51.

8. Ibid., 72–88. On the development of the notion of the sacrifice of the Mass, see Robert J. Daly, *Sacrifice Unveiled: The True Meaning of Christian Sacrifice* (London and New York: T. & T. Clark, 2009), 14–24 .

Thus, "the early Christian Supper always stood in a horizon of eschatological hope, that is, of future fulfillment as well as present experience."[9]
The age of salvation was associated with the fullness of the kingdom.
Later theologians would refer to it as the *eschaton*, though at its heart is
the root metaphor of the kingdom or reign of God. Originating in the
preaching of Jesus, the fullness of the kingdom was described by the
New Testament authors as good news for the poor, liberty for captives,
justice, and peace (Luke 4:18; Rom 14:17); as a new creation (2 Cor 5:17);
and as a new heaven and a new earth (2 Pet 3:13).

From Easter Hope to Fear of Judgment

Unfortunately, this vivid sense for Christ's coming to bring the blessings of the kingdom no longer informs our liturgical celebrations as it
once did. "The history of actual Eucharistic theology (its practice and
theory) demonstrates . . . the extent to which both the genuine remembering and anticipatory aspects of anamnesis have been obscured in the
East as well as West."[10] From the seventh century on, confidence in God's
mercy for those who had died began to give way to the fear of judgment.
Brian Daley attributes the darkening of Christian expectation to Gregory
the Great (540–604), who saw the chaos caused by the Lombard invasion
of Italy as a sign the Parousia and judgment were near.[11] Increasingly,
emphasis was placed on the purifying prayer of the church to free souls
from the fires of purgation, soon to be known as purgatory. One has only
to contrast the joyful exclamation of the primitive church, "Come, Lord
Jesus," with the *Dies Irae*, the thirteenth-century hymn once used as the
sequence at the Roman Catholic Requiem or funeral Mass. Full of the
fear of judgment, it looks toward that "day of wrath and day of mourning" when Christ who so suffered on the cross comes in judgment, a day
when "even the just are mercy needing." Hardly a message of hope.

---

9. John Reumann, *The Supper of the Lord* (Philadelphia: Fortress, 1985), 25. "At
every eucharist the church is in fact praying that the parousia may take place at that
very moment, and if the Father 'merely' sends His Son in the sacramental mode we
have at least a taste of that future which God reserves for Himself to give one day."
Wainwright, *Eucharist and Eschatology*, 67.

10. Bruce T. Morrill, *Anamnesis as Dangerous Memory: Political and Liturgical Theology
in Dialogue* (Collegeville, MN: Liturgical Press, 2000), 200.

11. Daley, *The Hope of the Early Church*, 211.

Joseph Jungmann has traced the different developments in the theology and liturgy of the West. The early church's worship was essentially corporate, dominated by the Easter motif that celebrated our victory over death assured for us by Christ's resurrection. The emphasis was on the divinity of Jesus, now reigning in glory. But by the ninth and tenth centuries a shift of focus becomes evident. The image of the glorified Christ began to fade, overshadowed by the image of the crucified Lord in biblical illustrations and on the panels of church doors. By the eleventh century it had become customary to place a crucifix on the altar, and a century later the crucifix or a crucifixion group became the dominant subject on the wall behind the altar. As the theme of the Last Judgment became more prominent, an increasing emphasis was placed on the individual—on human action, subjectivity, and moral accomplishment.[12] Pope Benedict XVI makes the same point in his 2007 encyclical *Spe Salvi*: "In the modern era, the idea of the Last Judgement has faded into the background: Christian faith has been individualized and primarily oriented towards the salvation of the believer's own soul" (no. 42).

As Christ's divinity was absorbed into his union with the Father, the notion of the church as the Body of Christ gradually faded. The church was described as the mother of all the faithful or as the Bride of Christ. The language of the liturgy was no longer understood by the faithful, the altar was moved farther away from the people into the apse of the church, and only the priest could enter the sanctuary. The church began to be represented by the clergy, who acted on behalf of the faithful, with the result that the "corporate character of public worship, so meaningful to early Christianity, [began] to crumble at the foundations."[13]

While Western theology became increasingly focused on the transformation of the elements, the liturgy of the East was more successful at preserving the ancient sense that to celebrate the Eucharist means to ascend to the heavenly sanctuary, to the table of Christ in his kingdom. For Russian Orthodox theologian Alexander Schmemann, the Eucharist is the symbol of the kingdom par excellence. Still, he laments what he calls the gradual narrowing, if not radical metamorphosis, of Christian eschatology. He argues that the church's worship was born and took shape "primarily as a *symbol of the kingdom*, of the Church's ascent to it";

---

12. Joseph Jungmann, *Pastoral Liturgy* (New York: Herder and Herder, 1962), 1–8.
13. Ibid., 58–60 at 60.

the Eucharist is the symbol of the kingdom par excellence.[14] The symbolic direction of the Eastern liturgy was one of *ascent*, while in the West it is more one of Christ *descending* onto the altar.[15]

Johann Baptist Metz also calls attention to a loss of eschatological anticipation in the liturgy. He asks, what is God waiting for? In spite of the response "until you come again in glory" that stands at the center of the eucharistic ritual, he questions whether the celebration is still a feast of expectation. Christianity has "detemporalized" its ideas of imminent expectation and the Second Coming. What is lost is the sense of awaiting, "while eschatology has been transformed into ethics."[16] The God of the biblical tradition is not bounded by historical time, Metz argues, but rather is to be described in terms of surprise, expectation, acceptance, and confrontation with the new.[17]

The Second Vatican Council

The Second Vatican Council (1962–65) took significant steps toward renewing both church and liturgy in its Dogmatic Constitution on the Church (*Lumen Gentium*) and its Constitution on the Sacred Liturgy (*Sacrosanctum Concilium*). Using biblical metaphors rather than the scholastic and juridical language of Vatican I (1869–70), *Lumen Gentium* describes the church as the People of God (chap. 2), the Body of Christ (LG 7), and Temple of the Spirit (LG 4). Thus its framework for its theological understanding of church is not narrowly christological but pneumatological and trinitarian. Its opening chapter speaks of the church as a mystery in which God calls all men and women to share in the life of the Trinity (LG 4), and it relates the church to the kingdom of God, already begun with the coming of Christ. Distinguishing clearly between the kingdom of God and the church, *Lumen Gentium* sees the church as the initial budding forth of the kingdom, revealed in the word, the work, and the presence of Christ and especially in his death and resurrection, while it looks toward its consummation when the church will be united

---

14. Alexander Schmemann, *The Eucharist: Sacrament of the Kingdom*, trans. Paul Kachur (Crestwood, NY: St. Vladimir's Seminary Press, 1998), 43.

15. Ibid., 60.

16. Johann Baptist Metz, *A Passion for God: The Mystical-Political Dimension of Christianity*, trans. J. Matthew Ashley (New York: Paulist, 1998), 85.

17. Ibid., 86–87.

with her king in glory (LG 5). Thus, the eschatological dimension is not absent, and it has a social dimension.

The Constitution on the Sacred Liturgy (*Sacrosanctum Concilium*) describes the liturgy as an act of Christ the priest and of his body the church, manifesting by signs the sanctification of his people (SC 7). Echoing the language of the churches of the East, it speaks of the earthly liturgy as a foretaste of the heavenly liturgy celebrated in the holy city of Jerusalem where Christ sits at the right hand of God (SC 8). Calling for the "full, conscious, and active participation in liturgical celebrations which is demanded by the very nature of the liturgy" (SC 14), the council fathers sought to retrieve the theology of the assembly. The liturgy is not the work of the priest alone; it is the prayer of the entire assembly (SC 33). This was to become clearer in postconciliar documents. The General Instruction for the revised Roman Missal (1970) returned to this theology of the assembly, as did the Catechism of the Catholic Church. Under the subheading "The celebrants of the sacramental liturgy," the Catechism states, "It is the whole *community*, the Body of Christ united with its Head, that celebrates" (no. 1140). To better express this theology of the assembly, the constitution stresses the importance of a diversity of liturgical ministries (SC 28, 29). It also calls for a simplification of the rites (SC 34) and, though somewhat hesitantly, for greater inculturation of the liturgy, a move that was to lead to the introduction of vernacular languages (SC 36).

The council's reform of the liturgy represented the most dramatic change for Catholics. Within a few years, that Latin of the liturgy had given way to vernacular translations. The rites were revised, needless repetitions and ritual gestures were removed, the presider now faced the people, and lay men and women proclaimed the readings and helped distribute the Body and Blood of Christ to the congregation as "extraordinary ministers of the Eucharist." Liturgical spaces were reconfigured, removing communion rails and the high altars, and new church buildings replaced the traditional long naves with designs that gathered the assembly closer to the altar and to each other.

Postconciliar Developments

While the council was largely successful in reclaiming a corporate sense for liturgy with its retrieval of the theology of the assembly, it is less clear that it brought about a recovery of the vivid eschatological imagination that so characterized the primitive church. At the same time, a number

of postconciliar developments were to lead to some very different challenges. They included a growing indifference toward religion, a more
informal, culturally-shaped liturgy, a new emphasis on the historical Jesus
in Christology, and a new direction in theology brought about by engagement with religious pluralism. The secular, postmodern ethos, so strong
in contemporary Western culture, has contributed to the decline in religious affiliation charted by a number of recent surveys.[18] It has also led
to a suspicion of universal truth claims and biblical metanarratives.

Religious Indifference

Building on his earlier study of teenagers, *Soul Searching*, Christian
Smith together with Patricia Snell in *Souls in Transition* profiles emerging
adults, those between eighteen and twenty nine years of age (though
the book studied only the first half of this group). Most are largely indifferent toward religion, though they see it as having a useful function, at
least for children, in that it helps them to be good and to make good
choices. Religious beliefs themselves do not seem to be important; emerging adults are content to determine for themselves what is right, worthy,
and important on the basis of their feelings and inclinations. Since no
one really knows what is true or right or good, it is best to remain tenta-
tive and keep one's options open.[19]

There are some negatives in the skepticism of many young adults that
leads them to decide religious questions on the basis of feelings or personal preference. Smith characterizes this attitude as the "cultural triumph of liberal Protestantism." Even though mainline Protestant
churches have been hemorrhaging members, he maintains that these
liberal Protestants have actually won at the cultural level, with an emphasis on "individual autonomy, unbounded tolerance, freedom from
authorities, the affirmation of pluralism, the centrality of human self-
consciousness, the practical value of moral religion, epistemological
skepticism, and an instinctive aversion to anything 'dogmatic' or committed to particulars." He sums it up by saying that many emerging
adults would be quite comfortable with the kind of liberal faith described

18. See Pew Forum, "U.S. Religious Landscape Survey," http://religions.pewforum
.org/reports.

19. Christian Smith with Patricia Snell, *Souls in Transition: The Religious and Spiritual
Lives of Emerging Adults* (New York: Oxford University Press, 2009), 286–87; see also
Christian Smith and Melinda Lundquist Denton, *Soul Searching: The Religious and
Spiritual Lives of American Teenagers* (New York: Oxford University Press, 2005).

in 1937 by H. Richard Niebuhr as being about "a God without wrath [who] brought men without sin into a kingdom without judgment through the ministrations of a Christ without a Cross."[20]

From an eschatological perspective, one of the beliefs that has been diminished or jettisoned is the sense that each of us must one day give an account of ourselves on the day of judgment (cf. Matt 25:31-46). According to Edward Schillebeeckx, contemporary "preaching is silent about hell, eternal damnation and judgment; they can no longer be heard from the pulpit."[21] Terence Nichols makes the same point in his book on death and the afterlife. He remarks that in spite of its being found throughout Scripture, today we do not hear much about God's coming judgment; instead, the emphasis is on self-esteem and feeling good about ourselves.[22] Pope Benedict XVI observes that our preaching is "one-sided," directed toward the creation of a better world rather than "the other, truly better world."[23]

A Culturally Shaped Liturgy

Postmodern culture, with its insecurity and sense of isolation, has also left its mark on the contemporary liturgy, often reshaping it in terms of its own forms and values. Commentators or cantors often welcome all before the priest processes in. Presiders too often adopt an informal style, starting with a joke or story or sometimes a ball score, welcoming all, often asking guests to introduce themselves. The talk is of welcome, celebration, ministry, and community. On the occasion of the twenty-fifth anniversary of the council's constitution on the liturgy, a 1988 Georgetown colloquium on liturgical renewal by the name of The Awakening Church focused on fifteen middle-class US parishes. Its contributors raised a number of questions about the relation between religion and society, liturgy and daily life. Aidan Kavanagh found the "gathering rites" of hospitality and inviting people into community that had

20. Christian Smith with Patricia Snell, *Souls in Transition*, 287–88; such a liberal faith is close to what he and Melinda Lundquist Denton described in *Soul Searching* as "moralistic therapeutic deism," though set within a wider range of alternatives (ibid., 155). See *Soul Searching*, 162–63.

21. Edward Schillebeeckx, *Church: The Human Story of God* (New York: Crossroad, 1990), 136.

22. Terence Nichols, *Death and Afterlife: A Theological Introduction* (Grand Rapids, MI: Brazos, 2010), 161; evangelicals constitute an exception here.

23. Pope Benedict XVI, *Light of the World: The Pope, the Church, and the Signs of the Times; A Conversation with Peter Seewald* (San Francisco: Ignatius, 2010), 179.

developed in many parishes to be more reflective of middle-class culture and a "therapeutic" ecclesiology. "There is no prayer or Godward direction in this new 'rite of gathering'; it is a set of activities not ritually very different from the same procedures used when persons of middle-class society gather for any purpose." He found little that was countercultural in the parishes included in the study, little sense of the assembly's transcendental solidarity before God in Christ.[24]

Monika Hellwig made similar observations. While more positive about the laity's ecclesial sense in the gathering rites and welcoming of others, she questioned whether the liturgy communicated a sense of service to society beyond the church, suggesting that what was needed was "a more political understanding of the redemptive and ecclesial task" that might "pit them against prevailing national and cultural values."[25] John Baldovin commented on the emphasis on intimacy and community, with the result that "people are tempted to look to liturgy for immediate gratification, noting that when communal identity is accentuated to such a degree, the element of mission is underemphasized" and worshipers are inhibited "from experiencing sacramental action as God's gift rather than their own creation."[26] He sees the challenge as one of helping those in the assembly realize that "the Eucharist is an anticipatory sign of the coming kingdom of God's justice and peace," with the implications of living out that witness on a daily basis.[27] If this sense of the coming kingdom has been lost, then the eschatological imagination has been severely diminished.

Joseph Ratzinger had been speaking out against what he calls the "negative sides of the liturgical renewal movement" long before he became pope.[28] In his 2007 postsynodal apostolic exhortation on the Eucharist, *Sacramentum Caritatis*, he spoke of the *ars celebrandi*, empha-

24. Aidan Kavanagh, "Reflections on the Study from the Viewpoint of Liturgical History," in *The Awakening Church: 25 Years of Liturgical Renewal*," ed. Lawrence J. Madden (Collegeville, MN: Liturgical Press, 1992), 87–89 at 87.

25. Monika K. Hellwig, "Twenty-Five Years of a Wakening Church: Liturgy and Ecclesiology," in *The Awakening Church*, 58, 67.

26. John F. Baldovin, "Pastoral Liturgical Reflections on the Study," in *The Awakening Church*, 104–5. In a later work he notes that "the talk show host approach" to Catholic worship is subversive of the liturgy's intent. *Reforming the Liturgy* (Collegeville, MN: Liturgical Press, 2008), 152.

27. Baldovin, "Pastoral Liturgical Reflections on the Study," 106.

28. Joseph Ratzinger, *Milestones: Memoirs 1927–1977* (San Francisco: Ignatius Press, 1998), 57.

sizing the grace and dignity with which the liturgy should be celebrated: "The simplicity of its gestures and the sobriety of its orderly sequence of signs communicate and inspire more than any contrived and inappropriate additions. Attentiveness and fidelity to the specific structure of the rite express both a recognition of the nature of Eucharist as a gift and, on the part of the minister, a docile openness to receiving this ineffable gift" (no. 40). His relaxing restrictions on the use of the Latin "Tridentine Mass" in his *motu proprio Summorum Pontificum* (2007) is part of an effort toward bringing about greater reverence in liturgical celebrations.

Shift to the Historical Jesus

In Christology, the focus has shifted from the Jesus of the gospels and the Christian tradition to the historical Jesus. In the hands of careful and balanced scholars—for example, John P. Meier, Raymond E. Brown, Walter Kasper, Elizabeth Johnson, and Terrence Tilley, to name just a few—historical Jesus research has contributed much to a greater appreciation of Jesus and his ministry, particularly to a recovery of the centrality of the metaphor of the kingdom of God in his preaching. Others, however, have used it to reconstruct the historical Jesus according to their own preconceptions. For example, the members of the late Robert Funk's Jesus Seminar claim to have discovered the "real" Jesus, hidden behind the theology of the evangelists and the dogma of the church. Funk takes the religious establishment to task for not allowing "the intelligence of high scholarship to pass through pastors and priests to a hungry laity."[29] While the Seminar's reconstructed Jesus, shorn of eschatology and the miraculous, has drawn a lot of headlines, the work of the Seminar has had little impact on mainstream scholarship.

Recently some scholars have begun to question an overemphasis on the historical Jesus. John P. Meier and Luke Timothy Johnson argue that what gets lost is the "real Jesus" or the "living Jesus." For Meier, "the historical Jesus is not the real Jesus, and the real Jesus is not the historical Jesus."[30] Given the paucity of sources and the fact that the evangelists were not able to record all or most of his words and deeds, the real Jesus is simply not available to historical-critical methods. The historical Jesus, while useful for theology, is a modern abstraction and construct, open to many

29. Robert Funk, "The Issue of Jesus," *Forum* 1/1 (1985): 8.

30. John P. Meier, "The Historical Jesus: Rethinking Some Concepts," *Theological Studies* 51/1 (1990): 14.

interpretations: social or political revolutionary, magician, proto-Pharisee, apocalyptic seer, wisdom teacher, or gay man.[31] Such a reconstruction cannot be the object of Christian faith. "The object of Christian faith is a living person, Jesus Christ, who fully entered into a true human existence on earth in the first century A.D., but who now lives risen and glorified, forever in the Father's presence." Access to this Jesus is given only through faith.[32]

Though his language is less measured, Luke Timothy Johnson's argument is similar. He argues that history cannot deliver a solid version of Jesus other than that presented by the gospels, that efforts of reconstruction lead to distortions of the methods belonging to serious historiography, and that the alternative Jesus offered usually mirrors the ideal images of the scholars themselves. "To concentrate on 'the historical Jesus,' as though the ministry of Jesus as reconstructed by scholarship were of ultimate importance for the life of discipleship, is to forget the most important truth about Jesus—namely, that he lives now as Lord in the full presence and power of God and presses upon us at every moment not as a memory of the past but as a presence that defines our present."[33] Pope Benedict XVI also is concerned that an overemphasis on the "historical Jesus" as reconstructed by historical-critical scholarship with its ever-finer distinctions of the layers of tradition has lost sight of the figure of Jesus himself. Though he accepts the historical-critical method as indispensable for reading historical texts, the starting point must remain the conviction of faith.[34]

A Revised Christology

Certainly the recent emphasis on the historical Jesus and the centrality of the kingdom of God in his ministry has been significant for Christian life as well as for Christian theology. God's salvation is far more than the promise of eternal life for the individual; the social dimension of Jesus' preaching is evident in the Beatitudes, the parables, the Lord's Prayer, and his concern for the poor. He preached about caring for the poor and abandoned (Luke 16:19-31), declared peacemakers blessed (Matt 5:9), and said that we would be judged on the basis of whether or

31. See Daniel J. Harrington, "The Jewishness of Jesus," *Bible Review* 3/1 (1987): 33–41.

32. Meier, "The Historical Jesus," 15–23 at 23.

33. Luke Timothy Johnson, "The Jesus Controversy: The Limits of Historical Scholarship," *America* 203/3 (August 2010): 12–13 at 13.

34. Pope Benedict XVI, *Jesus of Nazareth* (New York: Doubleday, 2007), xii–xxiii.

not we fed the hungry, gave drink to the thirsty, clothed the naked, and visited those in prison (Matt 25:1-45). In this way Jesus gave expression to the messianic themes of justice, peace, and reconciliation so important to the prophets.

The recovery of the historical Jesus is also important, *pace* Luke Timothy Johnson, if the church's historical christological faith is to be defended from the frequently heard accusation that later generations of Christians transformed the simple rabbi from Nazareth into a god, whether through the triumph of Paul's theology, or because of a hellenization of Christology, or simply through a mythologization. This was the point of Ernst Käsemann's famous 1953 Marburg lecture, "The Problem of the Historical Jesus," calling for a new quest in order to keep Christian faith and preaching firmly tied to the Jesus of history.[35]

But when combined with the current emphasis on religious pluralism, made more critical in an age of globalization, the new emphasis on the historical Jesus has frequently resulted in a significant revision of traditional Christology. For Edward Schillebeeckx and Roger Haight, Jesus is no longer the efficient cause of salvation, but rather its revealer or exemplary cause.[36] While acknowledging a certain tension between the historical and doctrinal aspects of Christology, Haight insists that Christology must begin "from below," with Jesus of Nazareth. The object of Christology is the historical Jesus.[37] From the perspective of soteriology or the doctrine of salvation, the story of Jesus is increasingly seen not as something Jesus accomplished, bringing about reconciliation and communion between God and humankind as in traditional soteriology, making him constitutive of our salvation, but as an example or model, showing us the way to God by his obedience to the Father and life of generous service. Haight writes,

> How did Jesus save? As revealer Jesus preached and actually mediated in his ministry the kingdom of God. This means that Jesus is an invitation to look for this process going on within the whole of

35. Ernst Käsemann, "The Problem of the Historical Jesus," in *Essays on New Testament Themes* (Philadelphia: Fortress, 1982), 15–47.

36. Edward Schillebeeckx, "The Religious and the Human Ecumene," in *The Future of Liberation Theology: Essays in Honor of Gustavo Gutiérrez*, ed. Marc H. Ellis and Otto Maduro (Maryknoll, NY: Orbis, 1989), 183–85; Roger Haight, *The Future of Christology* (New York: Continuum, 2007), 70.

37. Haight, *The Future of Christology*, 29–39.

human life and history. Movements aimed at advancing justice, reconciliation, and peace in the world, at resisting social suffering, have a sacrality marked with religious depth.[38]

Paul Lakeland is sympathetic to those who see Jesus more as the way to God than as redeeming us through some kind of metaphysical act. Salvation is about the quality and character of human life; too often it has been presented as "the blood sacrifice of a somewhat sadistic God, in which the death of Jesus ransoms human beings from their sins."[39]

If God's saving grace can be mediated through the story of Jesus, it can also be mediated through other religious figures and traditions. Jesus is seen as a unique but particular manifestation of God's salvation. He is no longer the universal savior, even if he is the normative one for Christians. In Roger Haight's words, "one must expect incarnations of God in other religious mediations analogous to what occurred in Jesus."[40]

Haight goes further to speak of an "uncentering" or "repositioning" of the resurrection in the structure of Christian faith. Without implying any minimization of belief in the resurrection, he argues that the central position of the resurrection, and thus of eschatology in Christian faith, makes it seem that Jesus in his earthly teachings and actions as a whole was not in himself a revelation of God: "Jesus' message is true, and his life a revelation of God, even if, contrary to fact, there had been no explicit experience of resurrection. Jesus' life, what he said and did, is the center of faith."[41]

While it is true of course that Jesus' entire life was a revelation of God, this "uncentering" or repositioning of the resurrection at least raises the question of whether or not the resurrection reveals not just our own ultimate destiny, the raising and transformation of our bodies, but also the transformation of creation itself (cf. Rom. 8:21). Has this revised Christology, in which the risen Jesus becomes one among other mediators of salvation, deprived him of his eschatological role of bringing the *eschaton*? Can we still affirm the incarnation of the Word as a unique event of God entering into an embodied relationship with creation through the person of Christ? Or is the Logos theology of John to be reduced to poetry, stripped of its trinitarian and cosmic implications?

---

38. Ibid., 71.

39. Paul Lakeland, *Church: Living Communion*, Engaging Theology: Catholic Perspectives (Collegeville, MN: Liturgical Press, 2009), 55.

40. Haight, *Future of Christology*, 162.

41. Roger Haight, *Jesus Symbol of God* (Maryknoll, NY: Orbis, 1999), 149–50 at 150.

Theology and Religious Pluralism

Since Vatican II, Catholic theology has been increasingly concerned to rearticulate Christian faith in the context of religious pluralism. This has been due at least in part to the council itself. Vatican II moved Catholicism beyond the old axiom of "no salvation outside the church" to teach the universal availability of God's grace (LG 16), and it brought Catholics to a new respect for the great world religions, teaching that the church rejects nothing that is true and holy in them; indeed, they often reflect a ray of that truth that enlightens all peoples (*Nostra Aetate* 2). The council's steps in this direction have been significant. A theological emphasis on religious pluralism has strengthened Catholicism for the task of interreligious dialogue, so important in the twenty-first century. Catholic scholars can enter into dialogue with a genuine respect for the religious Other, which makes dialogue a genuinely religious undertaking, open to the divine truth that may be reflected there. Without it, one attempts to dialogue with the presupposition that those who follow different religious traditions walk in darkness and error and cannot be saved.

The Federation of Asian Bishops Conferences (FABC) has developed an understanding of the church's mission in Asia as one of dialogue in the context of religious pluralism, and it has placed witness to the kingdom at the heart of its mission. In the FABC documents, religious diversity is seen not as something regrettable but as a positive value that represents a richness and strength, for God's spirit is at work in all religious traditions, and all represent visions of the divine mystery. The proclamation of Jesus Christ in an Asian context means first of all witness to the values of the kingdom; this is the first call of the churches in Asia.[42] The 1990 Fifth Plenary Assembly of the FABC pointed out that the challenge in Asia is "to proclaim the Good News of the Kingdom of God: to promote the values of the Kingdom such as justice, peace, love, compassion, equality and brotherhood in these Asian realities. In short, it is to make the Kingdom of God a reality."[43]

When the FABC met in Rome in 1998 for the Synod of Bishops for Asia, many of the bishops objected to the Roman-drafted *Lineamenta* or

---

42. Jonathan Y. Tan, "*Missio inter Gentes*: Towards a New Paradigm in the Mission Theology of the Federation of Asian Bishops' Conferences (FABC)," *Mission Studies* 21:1 (2004): 71–74; http://www.jonathantan.org/essays/Missio%20Inter%20Gentes.pdf.

43. Cited by Tan, "*Missio inter Gentes*," 81; see *FABC V*, art. 1.7 in Gaudencio B. Rosales and Catalino G. Arévalo, eds., *For All the Peoples of Asia: Federation of Asian Bishops' Conferences Documents from 1970 to 1991* (Maryknoll, NY: Orbis, 1992), 275.

outline for the synod as being too Western in its approach. While the *Lineamenta* took as its theme "Jesus Christ as unique Savior of Asia,"[44] many of the bishops objected that this was not a good starting point in an Asian context, with its religious diversity. They pointed out that the Roman document ignored the experience of their conferences in regard to evangelization. Their concern was *how* Christ was proclaimed, and they spoke of a "triple dialogue" with other religions, with culture, and with the poor.

Theologians such as Johann Baptist Metz, Jon Sobrino, Roger Haight, Elizabeth Johnson, Peter Phan, and Terrence Tilley have also placed witnessing to or "enacting"[45] the kingdom at the center of the church's mission. Though Peter Phan's missiological vision is always explicitly trinitarian, he argues that the mission of the church should not be seen as "ecclesiocentric," working to implant the church where it has not yet taken root, but as "regnocentric," witnessing to the kingdom of God, spreading gospel values—God's presence in Jesus bringing forgiveness and reconciliation, justice and peace throughout the world. In such a kingdom-centered ecclesiology, "no longer is the church considered the pinnacle or the very center of the Christian life. Rather it is moved from the center to the periphery and from the top to the bottom."[46] Like John the Baptist before Jesus, the church should say "the reign of God must increase, and I must decrease."[47]

For Haight and Terrence Tilley, the Christian mission is neither ecclesiocentric nor Christocentric, but theocentric; the goal is always God and God's reign.[48] For Paul Lakeland, the church's mission is oriented toward the humanization of society.[49] Such a regnocentric approach empowers the church to work not just with other Christians but with other religions

44. Thomas C. Fox, *Pentecost in Asia: A New Way of Being Church* (Maryknoll, NY: Orbis, 2002), 155.

45. Thus Elizabeth A. Johnson, *Consider Jesus: Waves of Renewal in Christology* (New York: Crossroad, 1990), 54.

46. Peter C. Phan, "A New Way of Being Church: Perspectives from Asia," in *Governance, Accountability, and the Future of the Catholic Church*, ed. Francis Oakley and Bruce Russett (New York: Continuum, 2004), 183.

47. Peter C. Phan, *In Our Own Tongues: Perspectives from Asia on Mission and Inculturation* (Maryknoll, NY: Orbis, 2003), 37.

48. Terrence W. Tilley, *The Disciples' Jesus: Christology as Reconciling Practice* (Maryknoll, NY: Orbis, 2008), 260; Haight, *Future of Christology*, 161; see also Schillebeeckx, "The Religious and the Human Ecumene," 186–87.

49. Lakeland, *Church: Living Communion*, 14.

as well. The church does not compete with other world religions for members, for God's grace is operative among all people of good will.[50] Seeing the church's mission this way also brings new clarity to our understanding of Christian discipleship.

The Vatican's reaction to these theologies of religious pluralism has not been slow in coming. The Congregation for the Doctrine of the Faith (CDF) has investigated the works of Haight, Phan, Sobrino, and Jacques Dupuis. Its 2000 declaration *Dominus Iesus* was drafted largely in response to Asian theology and its approach to evangelization. The declaration insists both on "the unicity and salvific universality of the mystery of Jesus Christ" (no. 13) and on the inseparability of kingdom of God from Christ or from the church (no. 18). Cardinal Joseph Ratzinger, under whose CDF presidency *Dominus Iesus* was issued, from the days of his study of Bonaventure has been strongly against what he sees as any effort to "immanentize" the eschaton, to use a term of Eric Vögelin.[51] That would mean for him, making salvation something *within* history, rather than *beyond* it, and reducing the church to a church of the poor, with a mission primarily social rather than one based on hierarchical mediation.[52] Ratzinger specifically rejects regnocentrism, an interpretation of the kingdom as a world of peace, justice, and respect for creation that can unite the different religions in a joint effort toward a common task. From this perspective, salvation becomes the work of human beings, a utopian messianism, not the work of God.[53]

Looking Ahead

These liturgical, christological, soteriological, and ecclesiological questions are all entailed in the doctrine of eschatology, the fullness of salvation revealed in the resurrection of Jesus. They cannot be separated or easily disentangled. The early Christians' confidence in God's salvation breaking into space and time and human history came strongly to expression when they gathered to celebrate the Eucharist. Jesus was the

50. Haight, *Future of Christology*, 142.

51. See Eric Vögelin, *The New Science of Politics* (Chicago: University of Chicago Press, 1952), 120.

52. See Thomas P. Rausch, *Pope Benedict XVI: An Introduction to His Theological Vision* (New York: Paulist, 2009), 53–54.

53. Pope Benedict XVI, *Jesus of Nazareth* (New York: Doubleday, 2007), 53–54.

"firstfruits" of the resurrection of the dead (1 Cor 15:20), promising a new creation. But God's salvation is inseparable from the person of Jesus (2 Pet 3:8-10). These questions will resurface in the pages ahead. But first, we need to consider three concepts that are central to any consideration of eschatology: creation, time, and memory.

Creation

The current tendency in Old Testament scholarship is to see creation as the horizon of Israel's faith in Yahweh who creates by word, by wisdom, and by spirit.[54] In the Genesis narrative of creation, placed by the postexilic Priestly editors at the beginning of the Bible, an all-powerful God brings order out of the primeval chaos, effortlessly creating the earth and its creatures, including man and woman created in the divine image and likeness, through the power of the divine Word (Gen 1:1–2:4a; cf. Ps 33:6, 9) and rests on the seventh day. This Genesis narrative still retains traces of the ancient Mesopotamian and Canaanite creation myths from which it borrowed.[55]

The older, second creation story (Genesis 2:4b to 3:24), which includes the Fall, links the human person (*hā ādm*) and the earth (*hā ādāmâ*) in God's work of creation. Shaped "out of the clay" (*hā ādāmâ*) of the ground (Gen 2:7), then differentiated as male and female (Gen 2:22), the man and woman are equal. They enjoy complete harmony with each other and with nature, as well as an intimacy with God. These gifts are lost through the temptation of the serpent to become "like gods" themselves. The earth is cursed and no longer freely offers its fruits, their nakedness becomes an embarrassment, the woman becomes subject to her husband, and they must leave the garden, no longer to enjoy God's presence there.

God's Wisdom and God's spirit are both strongly associated with a theology of creation, one that sees God's creative work as ongoing rather than as being something in the past like the Genesis creation narrative. The prophet Jeremiah attributes Yahweh's creative work to Wisdom (Jer 10:12), a theme developed further in the later Wisdom literature. Wisdom, begotten before the world was created (Prov 8:22-23), is present at creation (Wis 7:22; 9:9), "penetrates and pervades all things" (Wis 7:24), and

---

54. Walter Brueggemann, *Theology of the Old Testament* (Minneapolis: Fortress, 1997), 162–63.

55. John L. McKenzie, *A Theology of the Old Testament* (Garden City, NY: Doubleday 1976), 194–96; see Alexander Heidel, *The Babylonian Genesis: The Story of Creation* (Chicago: University of Chicago Press, 1951).

"governs all things well" (Wis 8:1). Proverbs describes Wisdom as playing in God's presence while God fashioned the world:

> Before the mountains were settled into place,
>   before the hills, I was brought forth;
> While as yet the earth and the fields were not made,
>   nor the first clods of the world,
> "When he established the heavens I was there,
>   when he marked out the vault over the race of the deep;
> When he made firm the skies above,
>   when he fixed fast the foundations of the earth;
> When he set for the sea its limit,
>   so that the waters should not transgress his command;
> Then was I beside him as his craftsman,
>   and I was his delight day by day,
> Playing before him all the while,
>   playing on the surface of his earth;
>   and I found delight in the sons of men. (Prov 8:25-31)

This Wisdom theology suggests that God's creative work is ongoing, not something that took place long ago. Furthermore, creation is for a purpose: that God might enter into relationship with humankind. Creation is the ground for covenant.

God's wind or spirit (*rûah*) is also involved in God's creative work (Gen 1:2), creating and sustaining life, for example in Psalm 104:29-30, a psalm that Brueggemann says is "perhaps the fullest rendition of creation faith in the Old Testament,"[56] a faith that cannot separate or keep distinct either Israel or creation in the future to be given by Yahweh.[57] The future promised will bring a new creation, an end of tears, and peace for all on God's holy mountain (Isa 65:17-25), a theme that will be taken up again in the New Testament.

For many more conservative Christians, Darwin's theory of evolution was seen as challenging the biblical theology of creation, and some have continued to wage war against it, rejecting it entirely or insisting on pseudoscientific theories such as "creation science" or "intelligent design" to "save" the biblical account, making it a source of scientific knowledge. At the same time, a great many scientists are nonbelievers, ninety percent of the 1,800 members of the National Academy of Science,

---

56. Brueggemann, *Theology of the Old Testament*, 155.
57. Ibid., 547.

according to John Haught. Both are guilty of a kind of literalism, refusing to recognize that the book of nature can be read at different levels, both scientific and religious.[58]

There is nothing about the theory of evolution that would necessarily rule out God's creative presence. Evolution and Christian faith in a creative deity are not incompatible. One is a scientific hypothesis, well supported with empirical evidence, describing how the diversity of living things came about. It is primarily descriptive. It cannot address the philosophical and theological issues of ultimate causality. The other, Christian faith, is rooted in biblical revelation. Pope John Paul II acknowledged in 1996 that evolution is "more than a hypothesis."[59] Ilia Delio notes that "a conference on evolution sponsored by the Vatican did not include supporters of creationism and intelligent design."[60]

Three further observations on the theology of creation are in order. First, we have a tendency to separate creation and eschatology, pushing both to opposite margins, to the beginning and end of time, thus losing sight of their essential connectedness. Linking the two is suggested by the Old Testament, which begins the story of God's saving work on behalf of Israel with the story of creation as the story of a God who saves, bringing the earth and its creatures, including men and women, out of the primeval chaos. The Yahweh who promises renewal and restoration to Israel from exile will also bring about a new creation. Similarly, in the New Testament St. Paul includes creation in the freedom from corruption that is the gift of Christ's salvation in its fullness (Rom 8:19-22). Thus, eschatology is creation completed or fulfilled—the return of all things in Christ to the Creator.

Second, creation is not some once-for-all event in the past. This represents Deist theology, which posits a divine architect or "watchmaker" who creates the universe and then lets it run according to its own laws; this is not Christian. Creation is ongoing, a *creatio continua*; without God's sustaining embrace, holding us in his hands in this very instant, we would simply cease to exist. Psalm 104 celebrates God's creative work, sustaining all creatures and providing for their needs:

58. John F. Haught, *Deeper than Darwin* (Boulder, CO: Westview, 2003), 13–15 at 15.

59. John Paul II, 'Theories of Evolution," *Origins* (December 5, 1996).

60. Ilia Delio, *The Emergent Christ: Exploring the Meaning of Christ in an Evolutionary Universe* (Maryknoll, NY: Orbis, 2011), 23.

When you hide your face, they are lost.
When you take away their breath, they perish
and return to the dust from which they came.
When you send forth your breath, they are created,
and you renew the face of the earth. (Ps 104:29-30)

The resurrection of Jesus marks a "new creation" (2 Cor 5:17; Gal 6:15); for Paul, the risen Jesus is the "last Adam" or "the second man" (1 Cor 15:45, 47). The book of Revelation sees God as preparing a new heaven and a new earth (Rev 21:1-5; cf. 2 Pet 3:13). These New Testament passages suggest a God whose creative power is actively at work.

Perhaps the greatest achievement of Thomas Aquinas was his doctrine of contingency. He described God as pure existence, self-subsisting Being, the only necessary being. God's essence is simply *to be*; it is pure existence. All else, all created beings have being only by participation; they are contingent, radically dependent on God, unable to account for their own existence.[61] Aquinas saw God working in all things as their first cause: "Since the form of a thing is within the thing . . . and because in all things God Himself is properly the cause of universal being which is innermost in all things; it follows that in all things God works intimately."[62] That is why God can never be discovered in creation; God is not an object to be observed and measured but a transcendent presence to be encountered.

Ignatius of Loyola also saw God working in all things. In the final meditation in his *Spiritual Exercises*, the "Contemplation for Obtaining Love," he invites the retreatant "to consider how God works and labors for me in all things created on the face of the earth—that is, behaves like one who labors—as in the heavens, elements, plants, fruits, cattle, etc., giving them being, preserving them, giving them vegetation and sensation, etc."[63]

Third, would a God who creates out of love abandon creation, including those creatures created in the divine image and likeness, allowing all to return to chaos or slide into nothingness, whether through sin or entropy? Classical theology has too easily separated creation and redemption, making the incarnation a "second step" to a creation gone

61. *Summa Theologiae*, I, q. 44, a. 1.

62. Ibid., I, q. 105, a. 5.

63. Ignatius of Loyola, *The Spiritual Exercises of St. Ignatius*, ed. Louis J. Puhl (Chicago: Loyola Press, 1951), no. 236.

awry. A classic example is Anselm's *Cur Deus Homo*, which argues that Adam's sin was an infinite offense, as it was a sin against an infinite being, and so the order of creation could only be restored by an infinite being making satisfaction. In Anselm's words, "God will not do it, because he has no debt to pay; and man will not do it, because he cannot. Therefore, in order that the God-man may perform this, it is necessary that the same being should be perfect God and perfect man, in order to make this atonement."[64] For Anselm, this is why God became man.

Such a conception is flawed from a number of perspectives. It reduces creation to an originating moment, focuses narrowly on Christ's death rather than on his whole life, ministry, and resurrection, and makes redemption depend on a transaction between humankind and God in the person of Christ. According to Gabriel Daly, "the doctrines of creation and redemption should be developed together and in a way which recognizes the feedback of one into the other. Salvation is not an afterthought; it is implicit in the creation of a truly free being."[65] Rahner's insight is correct: creation and incarnation are not two different acts but one, only conceptually distinct.

> We are entirely justified in understanding creation and Incarnation not as two disparate and juxtaposed acts of God "outwards" which have their origins in two separate initiatives of God. Rather in the world as it actually is we can understand creation and Incarnation as two moments and two phases of the *one* process of God's self-giving and self-expression, although it is an intrinsically differentiated process.

Rahner here is returning to a very old Christocentric tradition in which the creative Word of God establishes the world as the environment for his own materiality.[66]

Time

Eschatology is intrinsically connected with the concept of time. Because of the trinitarian nature of the divine mystery, God is both beyond

64. Anselm, *Cur Deus Homo* bk. 2, VII, in *St. Anselm: Basic Writings*, trans. Sidney Norton Deane (La Salle, IL: Open Court Publishing, 1951), 246.

65. Gabriel Daly, *Creation and Redemption* (Wilmington, DE: Michael Glazier, 1989), 54.

66. Karl Rahner, *Foundations of Christian Faith* (New York: Seabury, 1978), 197.

time and fully involved in it. As William Stoeger says, "while God in God's self transcends time and space, God in God's Word and Spirit fully enters temporal and spatial reality, first constituting it and then uniting God's self with it."[67]

But what is time? Poets tell us that time flows like a river, from the past into the future. The ancient Greeks had two words for time: *kronos*, referring to quantitative time, the chronological flow of events, and *kairos*, qualitative time, the opportune, decisive, or graced moment. Philosophers define time as the measure of motion. Modern science recognizes that time has no meaning apart from the material world; it cannot be completely separated from space and is dependent on the observer. Scientists prefer to speak of space-time; both are relative to material reality. Neither is absolute, nor are they ontologically prior.

For most ancient peoples, time was cyclic, a cycle of repeating ages or the revolving of the great cosmic wheel. The linear idea of time, that time has a beginning (creation) and looks forward to an end (eschatology), has its origin within the Judeo-Christian tradition. For the ancient Israelites, God's salvation was something that had happened in the past, in the great event of the exodus when God delivered the children of Israel out of oppression and slavery in Egypt and led them into a land of promise, commemorated in the Passover Supper (Exod 12:1-20). As Brevard Childs observes, Israel's cult, which replaced myth with history, set her apart from the general pattern in the Near East: "For Israel the structure of reality was historical in character, not mythical."[68]

Under the influence of several centuries of prophetic preaching, calling them to repentance, warning them of God's coming judgment, but also promising that God would not abandon them, Israel began looking forward to a new intervention of God in their life, for a messianic age, the day of Yahweh, and even the resurrection of the dead. Thus the religious imagination of Israel shifted to the future (Isa 43:18-19). For Christians, the age of salvation had already dawned with the resurrection of Jesus, and they looked, particularly in the Eucharist, for his coming at the end of time to bring the fullness of salvation and a new creation.

---

67. William R. Stoeger, "Faith Reflects on the Evolving Universe," in *Finding God in All Things: Essays in Honor of Michael Buckley*, ed. Michael J. Himes and Stephen J. Pope (New York: Crossroad, 1996), 177.

68. Brevard S. Childs, *Memory and Tradition in Israel* (Naperville, IL: Alec R. Allenson, 1962), 80.

Like the other Abrahamic religions, Islam looks forward to the resurrection of the dead and a final judgment, leading to eternal reward or lasting punishment. Modern Judaism does not have a single eschatology. Orthodox Jews look forward to a personal messiah in the Davidic line who will usher in a messianic age that will culminate in the resurrection of the dead. Conservative Judaism also hopes for a messianic age, though not always a personal messiah. As with Reform Judaism, some Conservative Jews see the messianic age as ultimately the responsibility of every human person. Buddhism does not really have an eschatology. With its unique view of time, without beginning or end and without a creator God, there can be no beginning in terms of creation and no end in terms of last judgment. If the word "eschatology" is used at all, it would be a completely realized eschatology because in the self-emptying and wisdom of Sunyata each "now" moment is realized as the eternal, and time is overcome.[69]

Modern science eventually accepted the originally Judeo-Christian religious notion that the universe, and thus time, has a beginning and an end. The theoretical physicist Stephen Hawking attributes this to Hubble's 1929 discovery of the expanding universe, leading to the big bang theory of its beginnings.[70] While most scientists accept this view, they remain divided on the ultimate destiny of the universe, though many accept that according to the second law of thermodynamics there is something irreversible about nature; the universe will eventually "run down," resulting in an eventual "heat death" or maximum entropy, a loss of the energy necessary to sustain motion or life.

Using a term originating with Arthur Eddington, Hawking distinguishes three "arrows of time." The thermodynamic arrow is the direction in which entropy or "disorder" increases; the psychological arrow refers to our subjective experience of time, remembering the past but not the future; the cosmological arrow is the direction in which the universe expands rather than contracts.[71] Thus, even if time is relative to the observer, it has a direction.

---

69. Masao Abe, "Kenotic God and Dynamic Sunyata," in *The Emptying God: A Buddhist-Jewish-Christian Conversation*, ed. John B. Cobb, Jr. and Christopher Ives (Maryknoll, NY: Orbis, 1990), 59–61.

70. Stephen Hawking, *A Brief History of Time*, updated and expanded tenth anniversary edition (New York: Bantam, 1996), 9.

71. Ibid., 149.

So too for the Christian community time has a direction; it is eschatological. As Don Saliers writes, Christianity "inherited from Jewish liturgy the rhythm of feasts and seasons in which God's mighty acts and the covenant promises of God for the future were commemorated." In the Christian Pasch or paschal mystery of Christ's passing from death to life, commemorated in the liturgy, we look forward to the fulfillment of God's promises.[72]

Memory

Memory brings time to mind and in recalling the past tells us who we are. Amnesia means the loss of memory, and with it, the loss of identity. Memory under various forms plays an important role in the biblical tradition. First of all, Israel continually remembered or reread its history in light of God's saving action in the exodus; this memory became, in Walter Brueggemann's words, the lens through which it retold all of its experience. In this way, God's powerful action on Israel's behalf was seen as entering into new situations.[73] In the same way, the earliest Christians, most of them Jews, reread their tradition in their preaching and texts to interpret the life, death, and resurrection of Jesus. They proclaimed him as Messiah, Lord, Son of God, Servant of Yahweh, as Word of God or Wisdom of God. Tradition itself became the living memory of the community, rooted in its originating experience of God's life revealed and made accessible in Jesus.

Most important is the concept of memorial, which gives an active sense to memory. From the Hebrew root *zkr*, to remember, or *zikkārôn* in the nominal form, "memorial" appears as the Greek *anamnēsis* in the Septuagint and later in the New Testament. What was remembered for the Israelites was the covenant between God and the people; to remember the covenant "was to allow the covenant to lay claim on their present reality. . . . Remembrance meant becoming aware of present obligations to remain faithful to God."[74] Religious festivals facilitated this process of remembering. Brevard Childs says that scholars today are agreed that "the chief function of the cult was to actualize the tradition."[75] For

72. Don E. Saliers, *Worship as Theology: Foretaste of Glory Divine* (Nashville: Abingdon, 1994), 53.

73. Brueggemann, *Theology of the Old Testament*, 177.

74. Richard Gaillardetz, *Teaching with Authority* (Collegeville, MN: Liturgical Press, 1997), 80.

75. Childs, *Memory and Tradition in Israel*, 75.

example, the Israelites were told to memorialize in the Passover Supper God's deliverance of the people from slavery and oppression, expressing it through narrative and ritual (Exod 12:14). At the same time, asking God to remember was to invoke his saving relationship with the people; asking him to remember his mercy or his covenant was "to expect him to apply it to things now."[76]

In the New Testament, *anamnēsis* was used in a similar sense in relation to the Christian Eucharist. The disciples were told to share the bread and the cup "in memory of me" (*eis tēn emēn anamnēsin*; Luke 22:19; cf. 1 Cor 11:24), that is, to remember Christ's sacrifice, "given for you" (Luke 22:19). Xavier Léon Dufour emphasizes that in comparison to the Pass-over, the event being remembered was now identified with a person.[77] Nils Dahl argues that in the early church the commemoration of Jesus' death and resurrection took place not in the subjective memory of the individual believers but in the celebration of the Lord's Supper. "The celebration itself . . . was a commemoration, an *anamnēsis* of the death and resurrection of Jesus where the history of salvation was re-presented by the sacramental commemoration."[78] For Edward Kilmartin, the members of the community join their own self-offering to that of Christ on the cross by participating in the celebration of the Eucharist, the corporate act of the ecclesiastical community.[79] Johann Baptist Metz refers to this as the "dangerous memory" of Christ's passion, death, and resurrection, which reminds us that his kingdom is coming; this is a challenging memory that calls us to conversion, inviting us into the mystery of his cross and resurrection.[80]

In a beautiful homily given for a woman killed in an automobile ac-cident who had been on the team that looked after the papal apartments, Pope Benedict XVI noted the relationship between liturgy and memory. He spoke of the paradox of singing the Alleluia at a funeral Mass: "This

---

76. Reumann, *The Supper of the Lord*, 289.

77. Xavier Léon Dufour, *Sharing the Eucharistic Bread: The Witness of the New Testament* (New York: Paulist, 1987), 112.

78. Nils Dahl, *Jesus in the Memory of the Early Church* (Minneapolis: Augsburg, 1976), 21.

79. Edward J. Kilmartin, *The Eucharist in the West* (Collegeville, MN: Liturgical Press, 1998), 360.

80. Johann Baptist Metz, *Faith in History and Society: Toward a Practical Fundamental Theology* (New York: Seabury, 1980), 90–91; see Bruce Morrill, *Anamnesis as Dangerous Memory*, 139–88.

is audacious! We feel above all the pain of the loss, we feel above all the absence, the past, but the liturgy knows that we are in the Body itself of Christ and that we live from the memory of God, which is our memory. In this intertwining of his memory and of our memory we are together, we are living."[81]

What the Pope suggests in his reflection here is that through memory and liturgy we are linked with those who have gone before us with the assurance of faith that their story is not over and done but goes on in that future that God has prepared for us. And this is indeed "Good News," Gospel (*euangelion*) for the countless victims of history, the millions whose deaths were often unwitnessed and unmourned. When we reflect on the twentieth century with all its bloodshed, its two world wars, its succession of genocides, it was a century of tears.

Conclusion

We have seen that the eschatological hope of the early Christians found strong expression when they celebrated the Eucharist; in fact, as Joseph Ratzinger argues, it is "inseparable from the experience of the presence of the final reality in the eucharistic feast."[82] But as the Easter motif lost its centrality and the church became less the Body of Christ and more the domain of the clergy, Christians began to focus increasingly on the Last Judgment, particularly in the West, and on the sacramental presence of Christ in the elements.

We need, however, to keep in mind Brian Daley's caution. The development of the church's eschatological faith was complex and somewhat cyclical: "Eschatological emphases in the early Church varied, apocalyptic hopes died and were revived, and individual or cosmic or ecclesiological or mystical perspectives succeeded one another not so much in a direct line of development as in response to the social and ecclesial challenges met by Christian communities in each generation."[83] But overall, the emphasis in the religious imagination of the faithful and their liturgical celebration shifted from the coming of the kingdom in its fullness, the *eschaton*, to the *eschata*, a more individualistic concept of death and judgment, heaven and hell.

81. Zenit, www.zenit.org/rssenglish-31144.
82. Ratzinger, *Eschatology*, 8.
83. Daley, *The Hope of the Early Church*, 3.

The Second Vatican Council made significant progress in renewing the church's liturgical life, but the postconciliar period witnessed a growing indifference toward religion and a tendency to introduce middle-class values into the liturgy at the expense of a sense of mission. At the same time, some new directions in theology have been both helpful and problematic. A new emphasis in theology on the historical Jesus has reclaimed his proclamation of the coming of the kingdom of God, and with it, the importance of eschatology not just for the salvation of the individual but for the coming of God's salvation in its fullness.

More problematically, the new context of religious pluralism has frequently led to a revised Christology in which Jesus appears more as exemplar than as universal savior, as well as to a new ecclesiology and understanding of the church's mission as one of witnessing to the kingdom, along with the other world religions, with the effect of separating the kingdom from Christ and his salvific work. While this regnocentric approach to mission has facilitated interreligious dialogue and offered a common purpose, uniting Christians with those from other religions, it also risks making the kingdom the work of human beings, reducing salvation to something within history rather than beyond it. It has also led to a new understanding of the church's mission, even to a decentering of the church itself.

Can the mission of the church simply be reduced to witnessing to God's reign, especially to the disadvantaged, without falling into the perennial temptation of liberal theology of reducing Christianity to ethics? And is Christ's eschatological role in bringing the *eschaton* at risk of being lost, as social betterment becomes the primary focus? We will return to these themes at the end of this book.

2

The God of Israel

In his monumental work, *A Secular Age*, Charles Taylor traces the gradual stripping of Western civilization of its mystery, its narratives of faith and religious practice, and ultimately its eschatological hope. He sees the process of abolishing the enchanted medieval cosmos as starting with the Reformation, with its emphasis on personal faith and its discomfort with sacraments, priesthood, and the sacred (in the sense that God's power is especially present in certain people, places, times, or actions), leading eventually toward the creation of a humanist alternative to faith.[1] The Enlightenment saw a slide toward the impersonal, with an increasingly secular modernity substituting Deism and Unitarianism for historic Christianity. God was no longer seen as interacting in history with human beings and the created order but had been replaced by an impersonal architect whose indifferent universe was governed by unchanging natural laws. From this perspective, Taylor argues that Deism can be seen as a "half-way house" on the road to contemporary atheism.[2]

The loss of transcendence meant that spirituality increasingly came to be focused not on God but on the self, on personal feelings; thus it was privatized and opposed to religion, which was now seen as institutional and impersonal.[3] God had become an impersonal principle or a

---

1. Charles Taylor, *A Secular Age* (Cambridge, MA: The Belknap Press of Harvard University Press, 2007), 74–77; see also Michael J. Buckley, *At the Origins of Modern Atheism* (New Haven, CT: Yale University Press, 1987).

2. Taylor, *A Secular Age*, 270.

3. Ibid., chapter 14, "Religion Today," 505–35.

"higher power," something like "the Force" of the movie series *Star Wars*, while many people today create their own religions, mixing beliefs and practices, claiming that they are "spiritual but not religious."

But the divine mystery cannot be completely banished from creation; it has a way of manifesting itself, intruding unexpectedly into our consciousness in moments of disclosure or revelation, like Freud's return of the repressed. Many of us have had the experience of intuiting something more, a graciousness in the world, a sense of wonder or presence triggered by nature or a gift of love or the bright face of one's child, or even hope in the mystery of goodness intuited in times of loss, suffering, and pain.

In this chapter we will consider how Israel's God, unlike the gods of their neighbors, was disclosed as a God who seeks out relationship with human beings, making a covenant with Israel. Through Israel's history, with its moments of triumph and tragedy, the God of Israel came to be seen as one whose saving acts are not just in Israel's past but increasingly lie in a future still unknown. Finally, we will trace how the eschatological and apocalyptic forms of thought that developed late in Israel's history helped the Israelites, or the Jews as they came to be known, to see that a God who was the author of life might also be a God who gives life to the dead.

The Gods of the Nations

From time immemorial humans have created gods in their own image or projected their insecurities and dreams onto an all-powerful other or others. The ancients worshiped natural forces or malevolent demons, the spirits of their ancestors, or the gods of their individual city-states. The inhabitants of ancient Mesopotamia and Canaan worshiped the god of fertility with elaborate new year rituals that involved sexual intercourse between the god and his consort, symbolized by the temple priest and priestess, with all the participants sharing in the ritual. Some practiced human sacrifice.

The gods of the Greek and Roman mythologies were anthropomorphic figures who governed the heavens, the seas, and the underworld, or personifications of natural or human forces such as love and war. Their veneration was supposed to provide some protection from powers beyond human control. Some of the gods of Mesoamerica were bloodthirsty deities whose cults involved human sacrifice. It is believed that more than one thousand victims per day were sacrificed over a period of twenty days when the sixth temple of the Temple Mayor in Tenochtitlan, the Aztec capital of what is now Mexico City, was dedicated in 1487. Neither transcendent nor "holy" in the sense of "righteous," these mythological deities were as capricious as the human beings whose virtues—and more often vices—they reflected.

Some ideas of the divine were more philosophically conceived. Traditional Chinese deities mirrored the stratified, hierarchical nature of imperial Chinese society; many understand them today as manifestations of the one Dao. As described by the legendary Chinese philosopher Lao Tzu, the Dao exists before the entire universe and generates the myriad things in the world, making it the "mother of the universe." The Dao itself is nameless, eternal, ineffable, unchanging, the source of being; it depends on nothing and cannot be represented.[4] Thus the Dao is the ultimate principle, though it remains impersonal.

Similarly, the ancient Greeks sought to identify the ultimate principle (*archē*) of all that is. Plato's God was *noûs*, or intellect, eternally contemplating the forms, though his ultimate principle seems to have been the Idea of the Good, which is virtually the source of the forms. The God of Aristotle is a self-enclosed deity, described as pure thought thinking itself. Neither creator nor personal, Aristotle's deity was a spiritual being, an eternal, cosmological cause or prime mover, posited to explain the world's motion but without contact with the world.[5] In David Knowles's words, "as his own being is the only fit object for his contemplation he has no knowledge of, or care for, the individual, and the whole machinery of the world is set and kept in motion by the love and desire that all being, consciously or unconsciously, has for God."[6] The idea of a personal God who might reach out to human beings in love and communion did not occur to the ancients.

Israel's God

4. JeeLoo Liu, *An Introduction to Chinese Philosophy: From Ancient Philosophy to Chinese Buddhism* (Oxford: Blackwell Publishing, 2006), 135–37.

5. See Alexander Sissel Kohanski, *The Greek Mode of Thought in Western Philosophy* (Rutherford, NJ: Fairleigh Dickinson University Press, 1984), 66–70; cf. Aristotle, *Metaphysics* 1072 a. 24.

6. David Knowles, *The Evolution of Medieval Thought*, 2nd edition (London and New York: Longman, 1988), 12–13.

One of the great lessons of the biblical tradition, expressed in many different ways, is the otherness or transcendence of God. This is a God very different from the mythological deities of ancient civilizations or from the abstract and impersonal first principles of the philosophers. It is a God who cannot be reduced to a scientific hypothesis or to a projection of human hopes. It is a God who remains mystery, beyond our imagining or even our understanding.

The transcendence of Israel's God, dwelling apart, dangerous even to gaze upon, is suggested in the Hebrew Scriptures by the notion of God as "holy." The idea of "holiness" (from the Hebrew root *qds*, meaning "separate") emphasizes God's otherness, difference, or apartness from all that is created, limited, and imperfect. Before the burning bush Moses is told, "Come no nearer! Remove the sandals from your feet, for the place where you stand is holy ground" (Exod 3:5). Even the holy name of God, YHWH, was not to be pronounced. In other words, God is the transcendent, the "wholly other," the holy—what Rudolf Otto calls *das Heilige*, the *mysterium tremendum et fascinans*, the mystery that is both terrifying and fascinating.[7]

At the same time, this God of Israel from the beginning has been reaching out to humankind, created in the divine image and likeness (Gen 1:27). Fundamental to Israel's experience is a God who, while remaining mystery, is also immanent and personal. Long before the Israelites knew God as Yahweh, their tradition identified God variously in relation to the patriarchs—the God of Abraham, the God of Isaac, or the God of Jacob. Thus the God of the Bible is a God who from the creation story in Genesis is seeking to enter into a relationship with humankind, symbolized by the man and the woman. This is a God who communicates, breaking the silence of his otherness and transcendence, speaking the divine word into space and time in his great work of creation and later in addressing his people through prophetic figures like Moses, Nathan, Elijah, and Isaiah who speak in the divine name. Thus the "word of the Lord" became a key concept.

As the God of a nomadic people, this God was not identified with a particular shrine or place but was seen as traveling with the clan or people. In the early Israelite writings, particularly those of the Yahwist tradition, God is described in anthropomorphic terms. According to the Yahwist tradition, God calls Abram from his country and his father's

---

7. Rudolf Otto, *The Idea of the Holy* (New York: Oxford University Press, 1958).

house and promises to make him a great nation (Gen 12:1-2), and Jacob in a dream hears God promising to be with him and make his descendants as plentiful as the dust of the earth (Gen 28:15).

As they settled into the land of Canaan, the ancestors of the Israelites encountered a universal deity, El (sometimes named in the plural form Elohim), worshiped under various names at different shrines. El Elyon (God Most High) was worshiped at Jerusalem, El Olam (God Eternal) at Beer-sheba, and El Berith (God of the Covenant) at Shechem. The Israelites often invoked God as El Shaddai, translated in the Septuagint as "Almighty" (Greek *pantokratōr*) or frequently as "the One of the Mountain." This mixing of religious cultures led Israel's ancestors to combine the personal God of the patriarchs with the universal God worshiped in Canaan. Genesis 49:25 joins these two traditions: "the God of your father, who helps you, God Almighty [Shaddai], who blesses you."

The proper name for the God of Israel was Yahweh, the name that could not even be spoken, written with the Hebrew consonants YHWH, introduced to the Israelites according to the tradition by Moses (Exod 3:13-14). The exact meaning of Yahweh is difficult to determine. Derived from the Hebrew root *hayah*, "to be," it is often translated as "I am who am," as in Exodus 3:14. Jerome translated it this way in the Vulgate. With its mysterious association with being, the God of Israel is the One whose essence is existence, simply to be.

The first eleven chapters of the book of Genesis, set at the beginning of the Bible by the fifth-century BCE Priestly editors, serve as a kind of overture to the biblical story or "metanarrative." They include stories of the creation, the Fall, and all that follows, and chapter 12 relates the story of the call of the patriarch Abraham and God's promise to make of his descendants a great nation, through whom all the peoples of the earth would be blessed (Gen 12:1-3).

While a literalist reading of these opening chapters—with its stories of creation in seven days, a tempting serpent in a garden of innocence, an escape from the great flood on an ark loaded with all the animals of the earth, and a tower aimed at the heavens—represents a decidedly unmodern credulity, a more sophisticated reflection reveals at least four highly suggestive themes.

God overcomes primordial chaos to create the heavens and the earth and all that is in them. Creation is good, the work of God's hands. The implication is that evil does not come from the creator but from somewhere else.

The man and the woman are created in the image and likeness of God, grounding the intrinsic dignity and value of each human being. They are destined for intimacy with God, who visits them "at the breezy time of the day" (Gen 3:8), and there is an innocence about them; they are "naked" and not ashamed.

Original innocence is lost when the couple succumbs to the temptation of the serpent to become like gods themselves, in other words, to become autonomous; they would no longer have to acknowledge God—the perennial temptation for human beings. What follows is murder, strife, the near destruction of the earth through the flood, and the division of humanity through the dividing of their languages; all of these are results of sin.

But God's will is always to save. In spite of the chaos that the man and the woman have let loose in the world—or more accurately, readmitted—God intervenes constantly to save, giving the man and the woman clothes to cover their nakedness, marking Cain to protect him from Abel's vengeful tribe, delivering Noah and his family from the waters of the flood and thus giving humankind a second chance, and promising a blessing in which all nations will share.

What follows in succeeding chapters and books of the Old Testament is the story of God's special relationship with Israel, combining history with its religious interpretation. God delivers the children of Israel from slavery in Egypt, entering into a "covenant" relationship with them, giving them the Ten Commandments, and leading them with mighty deeds into the land of promise, Israel. When they are unfaithful to the terms of the covenant, he sends prophets to warn them of his coming judgment but also continues to promise that he will not abandon them, repeating the promise, "I am with you" (Josh 3:7; Isa 41:10; 43:5; Jer 1:19; 15:20; 30:11; Hag 1:13; 2:4).

Covenant

Perhaps nowhere is the relational character of Israel's God more clearly expressed than in the biblical theology of covenant (Heb. *Běrît*; Lat. *testamentum*). Originating in the suzerainty treaties of the ancient Near East, these treaties or covenants governed political relations, listing mutual obligations and benefits. They were generally unilateral, imposed on a vassal by an overlord. While there are many examples of covenants governing social relationships in the Old Testament, the concept of covenant was adopted by the biblical authors to express the relationship between Yahweh and Israel. The tradition recognizes a number of covenants that Yahweh initiates: with Noah, with Abraham, with David, and especially with the people of Israel through the Sinai covenant, which remains associated with the dominant figure of Moses.

The covenant of Sinai was the basis of Israel's identity as a people. Rooted in the Exodus account of Yahweh's deliverance of Israel from oppression and slavery in Egypt, it found its clearest expression in the Decalogue, especially in the first commandment, "I, the LORD, am your God, who brought you out of the land of Egypt, that place of slavery. You shall not have other gods besides me" (Exod 20:2-3; cf. Deut 5:6-7). The "crowd of mixed ancestry" (Exod 12:38; cf. Num 11:4) that accompanied the Israelites out of Egypt found their unity in adopting the Yahwism of the Israelites. But it was Yahweh who initiated the covenant, entering into a personal, even filial relationship that made Israel a people. In his *Anchor Bible* study of covenant, Scott Hahn describes the Sinai covenant as one of kinship, a mutual relationship based on a joint commitment; it represents "a crucial theological adaptation of the kinship covenant, whereby a familial bond between God and Israel is established on the basis of a father-son relationship."[8] He cites D. J. McCarthy to the effect that "the concept of Israel's divine sonship in the Old Testament is often very like the concept of Israel, the covenant partner of Yahweh. Indeed, the two ideas are inseparable."[9]

Israel saw God's great saving work as centered in Yahweh's delivering the people from slavery and oppression in Egypt and entering into a covenant relationship with them on Mount Sinai, in other words, in something in the past, though they continued to celebrate God's saving action in Israel's life in the Passover Supper (Exod 12:1-27) and to praise God's work of creation and salvation in the Psalms.

The Psalter has been called the songbook of the Temple; its provenance is liturgical, giving us access to Israel at prayer. To enter the Temple was to come into God's presence. The Temple was the house of God to which the people joyfully processed (Ps 122:1), the place of God's dwelling in their midst (Ps 20:2), the palace from which God reigned (Pss 11:4-6; 18:7; 33:13-15), and its courts were the courts of the Lord (Pss 65:4; 92:14; 100:4). Reflecting the earlier tradition that God dwelt on the mountains, the Temple is occasionally called the holy mountain (Ps 15:1) or the mountain of the Lord (Ps 24:3).

---

8. Scott W. Hahn, *Kinship by Covenant: A Canonical Approach to the Fulfillment of God's Saving Promises* (New Haven, CT, and London: Yale University Press, 2009), 48.

9. Dennis J. McCarthy, "Israel, My First-Born Son," *The Way* 5 (1965): 191.

Sheol

But there is another, more somber theme that emerges in the Psalms, witnessing to early Israel's belief that covenant relationship with Yahweh did not extend beyond this life. With death the spirit (*rûah*), or principle of life and activity, departed and the self (*nepes*) descended into "Sheol," a synonym for death (Ps 28:1). Sheol was the underworld or abode of the dead; it was a shadow land (cf. Isa 14:9), a place of darkness (Pss 88:7, 13; 143:3) and silence (Ps 115:17). Going down into Sheol meant an end of one's relationship with Yahweh, a separation from God's love (Ps 88:5-13); no longer could the dead sing God's praise (Pss 6:6; 115:17; Isa 38:18). It was only much later, in the postexilic period, that Sheol began to be seen as a place reserved for the wicked, a tradition reflected in some of the noncanonical, intertestamental literature. In the New Testament, Sheol is sometimes referred to as the Greek "Hades" or more often as "Gehenna."

Terence Nichols references those texts that suggest a shadowy existence in Sheol, comparing it to the underworld as it is described in the writings of Homer.[10] In both cases, the dead are portrayed as unsubstantial "shades" (Heb. *rephaim*) who have lost their strength and life force, though they seem to have retained their identity and physical appearances. When Odysseus meets his mother in Hades and tries to embrace her, three times she slips from his arms, like a shadow or a dream. In the Old Testament, Saul visits the Witch of Endor in order to consult the dead prophet Samuel. When she conjures him up, Samuel appears as an old man and rebukes Saul for disturbing his peace, though he foretells Saul's coming death (1 Sam 28). The prophet Isaiah once taunted the king of Babylon with a description of his life in Sheol:

> The nether world below is all astir
>   preparing for your coming;
> It awakens the shades to greet you,
>   all the leaders of the earth;
> It has the kings of all nations
>   rise from their thrones.
> All of them speak out
>   and say to you,
> "You too have become weak like us,
>   you are the same as we." (Isa 14:9-10)

---

10. Terence Nichols, *Death and Afterlife: A Theological Introduction* (Grand Rapids, MI: Brazos, 2010), 19–23; see Homer, *Odyssey*, chap. 11.

Thus, in most places in the Old Testament, going down to Sheol really meant the end of life. However, Joseph Ratzinger calls attention to Psalm 73, a favorite of Augustine, where the psalmist prays, "Though my flesh and my heart fail, / God is the rock of my heart, my portion forever" (Ps 73:26). He sees this as witness that occasionally, without the concept of the soul or the idea of the resurrection, the idea surfaces from the experience of communion with God that the menace of Sheol can be overcome.[11] N. T. Wright also points to Psalm 73 as well as to Psalms 16 and 49 as "hinting at a future of which the rest of the ancient Israelite scriptures remain ignorant."[12]

Imagining God's Salvation

If the exodus remained the revelation of God's saving activity in the life of Israel, under the influence of several centuries of prophetic preaching both during and after the exile, when Israel had to wrestle with the question of Yahweh's faithfulness in the context of tragedy, evil, and death, the religious imagination of the people began to shift toward the future, toward a new saving act of God on behalf of the people. From this shift developed the biblical categories of eschatology and apocalyptic, as well as a new idea that God would raise the dead to life. Contact with Hellenistic culture also introduced another idea in the Wisdom tradition: the immortality of the soul. This idea appears in what was perhaps the last Old Testament book written, the Wisdom of Solomon (placed among the deuterocanonical books, called the Apocrypha by Protestants).

The process was not immediate. To sketch this shift in the Jewish religious imagination, it is necessary to review Israel's history, reconstructed from the Prophetic Books and later books written after the exile. Israel's national life as a united people was relatively brief. David, who became king of Judah around 1000 BCE, succeeded in uniting the southern tribes of Judah and Benjamin with the ten northern tribes, establishing the Jebusite city of Jerusalem, later called the City of David, as his capital (2 Sam 5:6-12). But the united kingdom did not long endure; it shattered

---

11. Joseph Ratzinger, *Eschatology: Death and Eternal Life*, 2nd ed. trans. Michael Waldstein (Washington, DC: Catholic University of America Press, 1988) 90.

12. N. T. Wright, *The Resurrection of the Son of God* (Minneapolis: Fortress, 2003), 107.

during the reign of David's son Solomon into the old divisions, with Israel in the north and Judah in the south. For a while both kingdoms flourished, but material prosperity for the upper classes, a series of weak kings, and the constant threat of religious syncretism led to a decline in the religious life of the people.

The Prophets

The prophets sought to call the people back to fidelity to Yahweh and the covenant. While prophetism was deeply rooted in Israel, it was a complex phenomenon, often divided into the "early" and "later" (or "classical") prophets. The early prophets included groups often called the "sons of the prophets" organized for worship, perhaps ecstatic, before the establishment of the monarchy. Included among them were seers like Samuel, whose role seems to have been both religious and political, and court prophets like Gad and Nathan in the time of David. The later or classical prophets, from Amos to Zephaniah, are those to whom an entire book was dedicated, though the book of Isaiah includes three different prophets covering the period from before (First Isaiah, Isa 1-39), during (Second Isaiah, Isa. 40-55), and after the exile (Third Isaiah, Isa. 56-66), that is, from 742 to after 515 BCE.

The message of the later prophets was primarily religious; they tried to call the people to conversion and the kingdoms back to their covenant obligations, rebuking the people for worshiping other gods, accusing them of infidelity to Yahweh and trusting in foreign alliances, frequently employing the images of adultery or harlotry for their apostasy (Hos 1–3; Isa 57:7-8; Jer 2:20; 3:2; Ezek 16:1-43). A common theme was the oppression of the poor. These prophets were not against the Temple cult, but they condemned a cultic piety that was not combined with conversion of heart and justice for the poor (Isa 1:10-20; 58:1-14; Jer 7:1-28). Repeatedly one hears references to the most vulnerable—the widow, the orphan, the stranger in the land (Ezek 22:7; Jer 22:3; Mal 3:5; Zech 7:10)—a tradition also echoed in the book of Deuteronomy, dating from the mid-sixth century.

The judgment that the prophets warned was coming was realized in 722 BCE when the northern kingdom of Israel fell to the Assyrians, followed in 587 BCE with the destruction of Judah, Jerusalem, and the Temple by the Babylonians, and the subsequent exile of the people. But the preaching of the prophets was never without an element of hope, variously expressed, that God would not abandon his people, that a "remnant would remain" (Shear-jashub, the symbolic name Isaiah gave his son; Isa. 7:3), ultimately to be purified (Jer 31:7; Mic 5:6-14; Zech 8:6-7, 11-12), that a new king, an anointed "messiah" of the house of David, would be raised up who would govern Israel wisely and bring peace and justice for the poor (Isa 11:1-9; Jer 23:5; Ezek 37:24; Zech 9:9; Mic 5:1-5). They spoke of the Day of Yahweh, when God's judgment would be revealed (Isa 2:11; Joel 4:14) and God himself would come again to Jerusalem with his holy ones (Zech 14:1-5). Ezekiel promised that God would renew the covenant with Israel (Ezek 34:25; 37:26), while according to Jeremiah, God would make a new covenant with the people (Jer 31:31-34).

The prophet known as Second Isaiah, writing toward the end of the exile, used the image of the exodus to prefigure a new going forth in the desert from exile in Babylon. In his "Servant Songs," some of the most beautiful poetry in the Hebrew Scriptures, he spoke of a figure who would bring forth justice on the earth, freedom to captives (Isa 42:1-9), and who would be a light to the nations, bringing God's salvation to the ends of the earth (Isa 49:1-7). But this servant of the Lord would suffer buffets and spitting (Isa 50:4-9) and be spurned and smitten, giving his life as an offering for sins (Isa 52:13–53:12). The figure of the servant is complex, a figure chosen by Yahweh referring sometimes to Israel collectively, sometimes to Cyrus, the Persian king who allowed Israel to return to their land (Isa 44:26), sometimes to the prophet himself. Pre-Christian Judaism read the Servant Songs from a messianic perspective; the New Testament identified the servant with Jesus, very possibly rooted in the example of Jesus himself.

It was this messianic expectation or hope in the prophetic preaching over several centuries that accustomed the people to look to the future for a new saving intervention of their God and in the process affected a shift in their religious imagination. This shift became explicit in Second Isaiah:

> Remember not the events of the past,
>   the things of long ago consider not;
> See, I am doing something new!
>   Now it springs forth, do you not perceive it?
> In the desert I make a way,
>   in the wastelands, rivers. (Isa 43:18-19)

It is interesting to note that some prophetic passages dear to Christians because of their Christological reference (e.g., Isa 7:14; 42:1-4; 53:13; 61:1;

Jer 31:31; Mic 5:2; Hos 11:1; Zech 9:9; 11:13), are generally excluded from the *Haftarot*, the Jewish lectionary read on the Sabbath and feast days.[13]

Eschatology

Much of Israel's salvific expectations remained within the context of history; God's salvation would be manifested through the historical process, sending a righteous king in the Davidic line, revealing his judgment against evildoers, coming to the rescue of the poor and the oppressed. But Israel's hope occasionally reached beyond the historical order and Israel's national life to a vision of a new order, a cosmic struggle, heralding God's dramatic confrontation with the powers of evil, bringing about a new creation, transforming nature, and introducing a new age of justice and peace. In other words, this vision was eschatological in the proper sense, a vision of the end times, particularly in postexilic literature, though some scholars see Israelite eschatology beginning as early as First Isaiah in the eighth century. A classic example occurs in Isaiah 11:1-9:

> But a shoot shall sprout from the stump of Jesse,
>   and from his roots a bud shall blossom.
> The spirit of the LORD shall rest upon him:
>   a spirit of wisdom and of understanding,
> A spirit of counsel and of strength
>   A spirit of knowledge and of fear of the LORD,
>   and his delight shall be the fear of the LORD.
> Not by appearance shall he judge,
>   nor by hearsay shall he decide,
> But he shall judge the poor with justice,
>   and decide aright for the land's afflicted.
> He shall strike the ruthless with the rod of his mouth,
>   and with the breath of his lips he shall slay the wicked.
> Justice shall be the band around his waist,
>   and faithfulness a belt upon his hips.
> Then the wolf shall be a guest of the lamb,
>   and the leopard shall lie down with the kid;
> The calf and the young lion shall browse together,
>   with a little child to guide them.
> The cow and the bear shall be neighbors,
>   together their young shall rest;
>   the lion shall eat hay like the ox.

13. See Hananel Mack, "What Happened to Jesus' Haftarah?" *Haaretz* (September 22, 2005; Elul 18, 5765).

The baby shall play by the cobra's den,
    and the child lay his hand on the adder's lair.
There shall be no harm or ruin on all my holy mountain;
    for the earth shall be filled with knowledge of the LORD,
    as water covers the sea. (Isa 11:1-9)

Notice how the first five verses look toward Israel's national life, to the historical moment when an offspring of David's father Jesse will come to govern Israel righteously, bringing justice for the poor and punishing those who do evil. But the second half of the passage shifts to the vague future, to a new era marking the end of history, a return to paradise when peace would reign even in the animal kingdom and all would know Yahweh as did the man and the woman in the primeval garden.

Similarly, the imagery associated with the Day of Yahweh shifts in the later literature from judgment in the historical order to a judgment that affects nature itself, darkening the sun and the moon (Isa 13:10; Joel 3:3), laying waste the earth (Isa 24:3, 19), ending the very alternation of the day and night (Zech 14:6), and manifesting God's supreme power over nature. Thus, eschatology can be seen as God's absolute future when God himself will establish a new order of justice, peace, and righteousness.

Apocalyptic

Closely related to eschatology is the genre of apocalyptic, originating late in postexilic Judaism. From the Greek *apocalypsis*, meaning "uncovering" or "revelation," apocalyptic literature offers a vision or revelation of a new order that transcends or breaks with the present order in a radical way. Usually mediated by a seer or visionary, apocalyptic literature relied on highly symbolic or allegorical language, usually involving catastrophic cataclysms with cosmic dimensions, attempting to imagine the unimaginable. Though often associated with the end times in the popular imagination, N. T. Wright, following George B. Caird, rejects the idea that apocalyptic necessarily meant the "end of the world" in the cosmic sense. Its vision was of the end of the present world order,[14] often occasioned by a society no longer confident of its own future.

Dermot Lane offers a helpful distinction between prophetic and apocalyptic eschatology. Prophetic eschatology announces a divine plan

---

14. N. T. Wright, *The New Testament and the People of God* (Philadelphia: Fortress, 1992), 298–99; see also George B. Caird, *Language and Imagery of the Bible* (Philadelphia: Westminster, 1980).

for Israel and the world aimed at changing the present social and political order. Central was the image of the coming Day of the Lord or Day of Yahweh. Apocalyptic eschatology is more cosmic and otherworldly; it looks to a vision or disclosure of Yahweh's sovereignty, a divine intervention that has little concern for historical developments; "all apocalyptic involves some eschatology, though not all eschatology involves apocalypticism."[15]

The "Golden Age" of Jewish apocalyptic extended from 200 BCE to 100 CE, thus embracing the time of Jesus and the early church. The book of Daniel (164 BCE) was the first major Jewish apocalyptic work; others included noncanonical books such as 1 and 2 Enoch, 4 Ezra, and 2 Baruch. These latter books are difficult to date. The majority of scholars date the various sections of Enoch in its original, mostly Aramaic version to 300–150 BCE. A later Greek version may have some parts composed in the early Christian era. A Jewish work, 4 Ezra dates from 90–120 CE, while 2 Baruch similarly dates from 95–120 CE. The apocalyptic tradition is important because it introduces the idea of the resurrection of the dead.

The Resurrection of the Body

The so-called Apocalypse of Isaiah (Isa 24–27) has a number of similarities to the apocalyptic writings. It speaks of the end of the world, with the Lord punishing the hosts of the heavens and the kings of the earth. And there is hope for God's people:

> But your dead shall live, their corpses shall rise;
>   awake and sing, you who lie in the dust.
> For your dew is a dew of light,
>   and the land of shades [Sheol?] gives birth. (Isa 26:19)

Though the passage is not conclusive evidence and some passages suggest similar wording in the context of a national revival (cf. Hos 6:2; cf. Ezek 37:1-12), many scholars see it as early evidence for belief in the resurrection of the dead, for the hope that God who created the heavens and the earth could also bring the dead to life. Nichols notes how this vision of the afterlife is different from that of Greek thought, not disembodied souls but "a vision of restored and embodied afterlife."[16]

---

15. Dermot A. Lane, *Keeping Hope Alive: Stirrings in Christian Theology* (New York: Paulist, 1996), 72–75 at 74.

16. Nichols, *Death and Afterlife*, 23.

The first clear evidence of a Jewish belief in the resurrection of the dead appears in the book of Daniel. Written during the persecution of Antiochus IV (167–64 BCE), Daniel reflects a time of crisis a little more than 150 years before the time of Jesus when Jews were dying for their faith. Antiochus IV Epiphanes, who had spent time in Rome as a hostage, was an enthusiastic proponent of Hellenistic culture, imposing it on his Seleucid kingdom, which included Palestine. Allowing a gymnasium to be built in Jerusalem led to a period of worsening relations (1 Macc 1:14). Finally, he outlawed Temple sacrifice, Sabbath worship, traditional festivals, and circumcision (the sign of the covenant). He ordered the burning of religious scrolls and set up an altar to Zeus in the Temple. While some Jews went along, those who resisted were subjected to terrible torture and death (1 Macc 1-2; 2 Macc 6-7), leading to the revolt led by Judas Maccabeus and his brothers.

The book of Daniel represents another reaction to the crisis. It counseled the Jews to remain faithful to their religion, reminding them that Yahweh was the master of history who would deliver the faithful from those who persecuted them, a theme obvious in the stories of Daniel at the court of Nebuchadnezzar, the three young men in the fiery furnace, Daniel in the lion's den, and Susanna. And in the context of martyrdom, with Jews giving their lives in order to remain faithful to the covenant, it testifies to the vindication of the righteous, to those whose names were found "written in the book," and to the resurrection of the dead:

> At that time there shall arise
>> Michael, the great prince,
>> guardian of your people;
> It shall be a time unsurpassed in distress
>> since nations began until that time.
> At that time your people shall escape,
>> everyone who is found written in the book.
> Many of those who sleep
>> in the dust of the earth shall awake;
> Some shall live forever,
>> others shall be an everlasting horror and disgrace.
> But the wise shall shine brightly
>> like the splendor of the firmament,
> And those who lead the many to justice
>> shall be like the stars forever. (Dan 12:1-3)

Belief in the resurrection of the dead is also present in other late Jewish works. It is present in 2 Maccabees (7:9, 14, 23; 12:44-45; 14:46) as well as in some of the noncanonical books mentioned earlier (2 Bar 49–51; 4 Ezra 7:29-37). According to N. T. Wright, by the second-Temple period, the early position that largely ignored the question of a future life had been reversed; by the time of Jesus, many either believed in some form of resurrection or knew about it as standard teaching.[17] Certainly the Pharisees believed in it, while others like the Sadducees, who accepted only the Torah as canonical, rejected it (Luke 20:27-38; cf. Acts 23:1-8).

The Souls of the Just

A different, more philosophical idea of life beyond Sheol appears in the book of Wisdom. The book was written in Greek in the last half of the first century BCE, most probably at Alexandria in Egypt, a center for Hellenistic culture in the ancient Mediterranean world with a large Jewish community. Though used by the early church, the book of Wisdom was not included in the Jewish canon and so was dropped from the Protestant Old Testament canon by the Reformers in the sixteenth century. It describes the souls of the just as resting in the presence of God. The use of the term "soul" reflects Hellenistic culture, evident also in the Jewish intertestamental literature.

> But the souls of the just are in the hands of God,
>   and no torment shall touch them.
> They seemed, in the view of the foolish, to be dead;
>   and their passing away was thought an affliction
>   and their going forth from us, utter destruction.
> But they are in peace.
> For if before men, indeed, they be punished,
>   yet is their hope full of immortality;
> Chastised a little, they shall be greatly blessed,
>   because God tried them
>   and found them worthy of himself.
> As gold in the furnace, he proved them,
>   and as sacrificial offerings he took them to himself. (Wis 3:1-6)

Nichols notes that this passage differs from Platonism in two respects. First, the souls of the just are in the hands of God, not because they are immortal by nature as Plato held, but because of God's grace. Second, verse 8, which says, "They will govern nations and rule over peoples,"

---

17. Wright, *The Resurrection of the Son of God*, 129.

Nichols suggests, "may refer to the resurrected state, not to a state of discarnate immortality."[18] Thus Wisdom's theology, in spite of the influence of Hellenistic thought, remains firmly Jewish. In Roland Murphy's words, "immortality is not rooted in the human makeup, but in one's relationship to God."[19]

The Last Judgment

The idea of the Last Judgment has its roots in the Old Testament idea of the coming Day of the Lord, though the concept has a range of meanings. While the Day of Yahweh or Day of the Lord may have originally referred to God's saving intervention on behalf of his people, as at the exodus, the idea first appears in a negative sense in the prophet Amos, where the prophet associates it with the fall of Israel. It will be a day of darkness and gloom (Amos 5:18-20). It appears again in Isaiah 2:11-20, where it is broadened to include others in God's judgment against the proud, the arrogant, and those who worship idols, taking on a cosmic dimension, with the sun and moon darkened and the stars not sending forth their light (Isa 3:9-10).

In postexilic eschatology, using images that would reappear in the medieval hymn *Dies Irae*, the Day of the Lord will be a day of destruction and desolation, consuming the earth in fire, subjecting all the earth to God's judgment (Zeph 1-2). Joel 4:14-21 echoes this cosmic imagery but also sees the Lord's judgment falling on the nations, while promising vindication for Israel. Zechariah 14 offers a similar vision. These prophetic texts look forward to a decisive intervention or judgment of Yahweh, sometimes cloaked in cosmic imagery, affecting not just Israel as a nation but all the nations. Thus the Day of the Lord has a nationalistic connotation. It is more than a judgment against Israel for her infidelity or against the nations that oppress her; it also means security, peace, and restoration for God's people as God manifests the divine righteousness.

It is under the influence of Jewish apocalyptic that the idea enters the tradition that there will be a judgment after death, a last judgment. Daniel 12:1-3 suggests that it is the righteous Jews who will be raised to life, with the implication of some kind of judgment at the "end of days" (Dan 12:13). Similarly, the passage from Wisdom implies a judgment, in

---

18. Nichols, *Death and Afterlife*, 28.

19. Roland E. Murphy, *The Tree of Life: An Exploration of the Wisdom Literature*, 3rd ed. (Grand Rapids, MI: William B. Eerdmans, 1990), 86.

speaking of God's testing the just to find them worthy (Wis 3:5). The idea of a final or last judgment becomes much stronger in the apocalyptic literature, along with a number of developments of the concept of Sheol we considered earlier. First, according to D. S. Russell's analysis of late Jewish apocalyptic literature, the dead are no longer described as "shades" but as "souls" or "spirits" who survive as individual, conscious beings. There is a continuity between the present life and the next, so that these souls or spirits can maintain a fellowship with God beyond the grave and experience various emotions (2 Esdr [or 4 Ezra] 7:80ff.).

Second, the dead are separated into moral categories, the wicked and the righteous, on the basis of the choices they made in life (2 Bar 54:15; cf. 51:16), a distinction first made in the book of Daniel. While some books recognize the possibility of a moral change for those in Sheol through intercessory prayer (cf. Apoc of Moses 35:2), the majority see no change possible after death.

Third, Sheol is regarded as an intermediate state where the dead await the resurrection and final judgment. It has become a place of preliminary rewards and punishment, from which no progress is possible (2 Esdr 7). In a few books, it is the place of final judgment. Finally, Sheol has different compartments to accommodate both the righteous and sinners, some of whom must still receive punishment for their sins (1 Enoch 22). Found here is the first reference to the idea of a place of torment, hell, though the word itself is not used.[20] There are also different visions of the body for those raised up in these books; sometimes it is to a renewed earthly life, but in other works the body is transformed, prefiguring the idea found in the New Testament.

Conclusion

From a theological perspective, the God of the Bible is a God who from the beginning is seeking to enter into a relationship with humankind, symbolized by the man and the woman in the Genesis creation stories and by the story of Israel that follows. Unlike the gods of their neighbors, gods based on natural forces or political mythologies, Israel's God was transcendent, something suggested by the very name of Yahweh, a God

---

20. D. S. Russell, *The Method and Message of Jewish Apocalyptic* (Philadelphia: Westminster, 1964), 357–65. For a fuller discussion, see Nichols, *Death and Afterlife*, 29–32.

beyond all imagining, in spite of the occasional use of anthropomorphic language. The Torah forbad making images of Yahweh (Exod 20:4; cf. Deut 5:8; cf. Lev 26:1); none have ever been found.

But this God was also immanent, active in history, present to creation. This God was characterized by compassion and love, a God described at times with maternal images as one who gave birth to Israel (Deut 32:18), remembering Zion as a mother remembers with tenderness the child of her womb (Isa 49:15; cf. 66:13). This God hears the cry of the poor (Exod 22:22, 26), forbidding the "second picking" of the fields at harvest time so that the poor might have something to eat (Deut 24:19-21). Thus Israel's God is a God who communicates, breaking the silence of the divine otherness and transcendence, speaking the divine word into space and time and human history.

This God first appears in history as a Semitic tribal deity, the God of Abraham, Isaac, and Jacob, a God who travelled with the people chosen to be his own, later manifesting himself in what Israel would ever after celebrate at Passover as a great work of redemption, leading them out of slavery and oppression, entering into a personal relationship with them expressed in the Sinai covenant, making them a nation, a people, even the Lord's firstborn son (Exod 4:22).

Something of the joy the children of Israel experienced in their covenant relationship with the one they called Yahweh or the Lord can be felt even today in the Psalms. They entered his house with songs and rejoicing, recited the story of his saving works of creation and redemption, and turned to him in times of sorrow and lamentation. Their relationship with their God was real and vital, though for much of their history it was without any idea of a life with God beyond the grave, which brought that relationship with God to a close, for there was no worship or praise of God in Sheol.

Like all national stories, Israel's history knew moments of triumph as well as tragedy, and as the people wrestled with sin, national failure, and the humiliation of exile, the prophets assured them of God's faithfulness to his covenant people and promised a new manifestation of his saving grace, variously imagined, in a future still unknown. This expectation of a future intervention of God on Israel's behalf, reaching beyond history, introduces the category of eschatology.

Still later, the apocalyptic tradition, including a number of noncanonical works, looked forward to a dramatic, even cosmic, end to the present age and included the idea of the resurrection of the dead. First present in the book of Daniel, it may well reflect a time when Jews were being martyred for fidelity to their faith and began asking, can the God who is the giver of life also give life to the dead? Much of what would later characterize the popular Christian eschatological imagination originates in these and other apocalyptic books: the resurrection of the dead (Dan 12:1-3), the idea that souls survive after death (2 Esdr 7:80), that each person would face a judgment (1 Enoch 22), and that the righteous would be separated from the wicked before the final judgment and general resurrection (2 Bar 54:15).

The Wisdom tradition, developing in the period after the exile, pondered the mystery of suffering and death, particularly the plight of the righteous whose suffering seems unjust and unrecompensed. The book of Job, an early meditation on this theme, ends (after Job eloquently demands to know the reason for his sufferings) by affirming the incomprehensibility of the divine mystery (Job 38-39). Ecclesiastes is pessimistic; it holds that both the wise person and the fool will perish, for "all is vanity and a chase after the wind" (Eccl 2:17). But the very late book of Wisdom expresses confidence that the souls of the just are in the hands of God. Thus Old Testament wisdom broke down the ancient idea that God rewards the good and punishes the evil in this life, a view so contrary to our own experience, suggesting that God would come to the rescue of the just (Wis 2:20).

3

The Way of Jesus

The way of Jesus has been differently understood and expressed in Christian history. Influenced by cultural changes, theological developments, and historical movements, it has sometimes moved in directions not fully consonant with the message of Jesus, with the "good news" he preached. Jesus himself called men and women to himself as disciples (*mathētēs*), challenging them to "follow after" (*akolouthēn*) him. As early as Paul, the concept of following Jesus was expressed by the concept of *mimesis* (imitation), though the two concepts were not identical, "since following (*sequi*) implied coming after and responding to an appeal, while imitation (*imitare*) involved the idea of confirming and identifying."[1] Paul says, "Be imitators of me, as I am of Christ" (1 Cor 11:1; cf. 1 Thess 1:6).

The earliest name for the Jesus movement seems to have been "the Way," a term also used by the community at Qumran to describe their life. The Acts of the Apostles speaks of the early Christians as instructed in "the Way of the Lord" (Acts 18:25) or "the Way [of God]" (Acts 18:26), and it simply uses "the Way" to characterize their way of life (Acts 19:23; cf. Acts 9:2; 19:9, 23; 22:4; 24:14, 22). A similar usage seems to be present in Mark, where "the way" serves as an inclusion joining the material between Mark 8:27 and 10:52 with a lesson of Jesus on discipleship, broken into three sections; each involves a prediction of the passion, a misunderstanding by the disciples, and an instruction on the true nature of discipleship. The way of Jesus involves suffering and the cross; it

---

1. Giles Constable, *Three Studies in Medieval Religious and Social Thought* (New York: Cambridge University Press, 1995), 146.

means taking the last place and being the servant of all, "for the Son of Man did not come to be served but to serve and to give his life as a ransom for many" (Mark 10:45). It also involves compassionate service of others, healing the sick, driving out evil spirits, and preaching good news to the poor. It means embracing the paschal mystery. In the Gospel of John, Jesus says simply, "I am the way and the truth and the life" (John 14:6).

In this chapter, we will investigate what it means to follow Jesus as this was understood in his ministry, in Scripture, and in subsequent Christian history. Finally, we will consider some new insights from recent scholarship into what it means to follow Jesus.

Following Jesus

There were two religious movements in Palestinian Judaism at the time of Jesus: that of the Pharisees, still in its initial stage, and that of Jesus. How should we understand the Jesus movement? The Jesus of history was not just a wandering wisdom teacher or sage, as some contemporary scholars such as those in the controversial Jesus Seminar argue. He was not a revolutionary who appealed to struggle or violence against the occupying Romans, nor was he a social reformer, arguing against the "politics of purity." Still less was he a leader of the poor against the upper classes. Jesus was part of the religious community of Israel, familiar with the prophets who preceded him, brought up in the traditions of his people. The fact that he chose "the Twelve" and placed them at the center of his movement shows that he saw himself as establishing a renewed or eschatological Israel, the Israel of salvation.

Luke especially highlights his ministry to the poor. At the beginning of his gospel he sees Jesus as applying to himself the words of Isaiah 61:1-2, with their strong emphasis on his ministry to the poor. The passage reads,

> "The Spirit of the Lord is upon me,
>   because he has anointed me
>   to bring glad tidings to the poor.
> He has sent me to proclaim liberty to captives
>   and recovery of sight to the blind,
>   to let the oppressed go free,
>   and to proclaim a year acceptable to the Lord." (Luke 4:18)

Three themes running through the Synoptic tradition offer an insight into Jesus' intentions; he holds up the vision of a new family, invites men and women to follow him as disciples, and proclaims the coming of the kingdom of God.

A New Family

The metaphor of a new family runs throughout the Synoptic tradition.[2] When the mother and brothers of Jesus come seeking him, he replies, "Who are my mother and [my] brothers? . . . Here are my mother and my brothers. [For] whoever does the will of God is my brother and sister and mother" (Mark 3:33-34). This suggests a new family based not on clan, kinship, or patriarchy but rather on the acceptance of the kingdom of God. From the cross he entrusts his mother to the Beloved Disciple, to be his mother, another powerful sign of the new family of disciples (John 19:26-27).

Many of Jesus' sayings about this new family run against the grain of the patriarchal culture of the East. For example, he says, "If anyone comes to me without hating his father and mother, wife and children, brothers and sisters, even his own life, he cannot be my disciple" (Luke 14:26; cf. Matt 10:37). When a certain man begged to leave to bury his father, a basic familial responsibility, before following him, Jesus said, "Let the dead bury their dead. But you, go and proclaim the kingdom of God" (Luke 9:60; cf. Matt 8:22). Jesus was not unaware of the conflict his call would occasion:

> For I have come to set
>   a man "against his father,
>   a daughter against her mother,
>   and a daughter-in-law against her mother-in-law;
>   and one's enemies will be those of his household." (Matt 10:35-36)

Being a member of this new family was not without cost. The same was true for being a disciple.

Discipleship

Throughout his ministry Jesus was accompanied by a group of disciples. The word "disciple" appears more than 250 times in the New

2. Richard A. Horsley, *Sociology and the Jesus Movement* (New York: Continuum, 1994), 122–24.

Testament, mostly in the gospels and Acts. The Jesus movement was constituted by the disciples who followed him. And while the institution of discipleship was not unknown to Rabbinic Judaism, there were a number of unique features to being a disciple of Jesus. First, one did not choose to be a disciple; the invitation came from Jesus. Second, being a disciple of Jesus meant a radical break with the past. Those who followed Jesus "left everything" (Luke 5:11). They left behind parents, family, children, and jobs (Luke 14:26; Mark 2:14). They shared Jesus' poverty and itinerant life (Matt 8:20). For some it involved celibacy for the sake of the kingdom (Matt 19:11-12). Third, there was an inclusive character to Jesus' call to discipleship; it was not restricted to the ritually pure, to the religiously observant, or to men. There were "tax collectors and sinners" among the disciples (Mark 2:15) as well as some women (Luke 8:2), even if the Greek feminine for disciple, *mathēria*, was never used in the gospels, probably out of respect for the relatively fixed gospel tradition.[3]

Most of all, being a disciple of Jesus did not mean simply learning and passing on his teaching, as in the case of the disciples of the Pharisees. Being a disciple of Jesus meant sharing in his ministry. They are to share what they have with others (Luke 6:30), be willing to take the place of a slave, serving others as Jesus did (Mark 10:44-45), and bear insult and injury (Matt 5:38-42). Jesus sent them out to heal the sick, cast out demons, and proclaim that the kingdom of God was at hand (Mark 6:7-13; Luke 9:6; 10:2-12)—in other words, to do what Jesus himself was doing. Thus, to be a disciple of Jesus was to be at the service of the kingdom.

The Kingdom of God

The kingdom or reign of God (*basileia tou theou*) was the metaphor at the center of the preaching of Jesus. Even though he may have been the first to coin and regularly use the expression, it would have been familiar to those who heard him, all of them Jews. The phrase "kingdom of God" occurs over 150 times in the New Testament, most often in the Synoptic Gospels, but its roots lie deep in the Old Testament in the concept of the kingship of Yahweh. To speak of God as king is to speak of a dynamic reality, God exercising his creative, saving power over Israel, the nations,

3. See John P. Meier, *A Marginal Jew*, vol. 3, *Companions and Competitors* (New York: Doubleday, 2001), 73–79.

and creation itself, a theme taken up frequently in the Psalms (Pss 22:29; 47; 74:12; 93; 95–99). The theme appears again in the late Old Testament period (Tob 13:1; Dan 3:54; Wis 10:10) and in the Jewish intertestamental literature, where God's kingdom or reign is associated with apocalyptic displays of power and judgment.

Though many of Jesus' parables are centered on the kingdom, he does not explain it; rather, he acts it out. Better translated as the "reign of God," the kingdom is a dynamic event, God's saving action mediated through the ministry of Jesus. The kingdom is already at hand, being realized in the ministry of Jesus, evidenced in his miracles, exorcisms, table fellowship, and proclamation of the forgiveness of sins. One of the clearest texts is Luke 11:20, where, in response to the criticism of his opponents that he drove out evil spirits by the power of Beelzebul, Jesus responds, "if it is by the finger of God that [I] drive out demons, then the kingdom of God has come upon you."

Kenan Osborne offers the following substitutes for the phrase "kingdom of God"; it refers to God's presence, love, compassion, mercy, power, forgiveness, justice, holiness, goodness, creativeness, grace, and relatedness.[4] Many see Jesus' ministry as the initial realization of the messianic age when God's justice and salvation would be revealed. Others see the kingdom as an apocalyptic idea: "God's power of justice, mercy, and love is coming into the world of oppression, fear, sickness, and sin, the world ruled by Satan (in the New Testament's view)." It means also "a reversal of social status: the rich and powerful will be put down and the lowly exalted," as we see in the Beatitudes and the woes of Luke's Sermon on the Plain (Luke 6:20-25).[5]

There remains a future dimension to the kingdom, illustrating its eschatological nature. Jesus taught his disciples in the Lord's Prayer to pray "your kingdom come" (Matt 6:10; Luke 11:2). He emphasized that the kingdom was present and yet not fully realized in parables like the weeds among the wheat, the mustard seed, the yeast in the flour, and the net cast into the sea (Matt 13:24-50). And he spoke of the Son of Man coming in glory to judge all the nations (Matt 25:31-46; cf. 26:64; cf. Luke 17:22-24). Did the coming of the kingdom include the resurrection of the dead? Did Jesus himself believe in the resurrection? There are good

---

4. Kenan B. Osborne, *The Resurrection of Jesus: New Considerations for Its Theological Interpretation* (New York: Paulist, 1997), 150.

5. Terence Nichols, *Death and Afterlife: A Theological Introduction* (Grand Rapids, MI: Brazos, 2010), 36.

reasons for judging that he did, as did the Pharisees in his day (Mark 12:18-27). As Brian Robinette observes, teaching about the resurrection or any form of life after death is absent from the Torah, which was why the more conservative Sadducees, who did not include in their canon the Prophets or Writings, rejected it. "Jesus shows that the resurrection is entirely in keeping with the Torah. The creator-covenant God who brings new life out of exile will surely not leave humanity abandoned to the ultimate exile of death."[6]

At the same time, as Dermot Lane argues, the eschatology of Jesus is not simply otherworldly, purely spiritual, or nonpolitical. It has a social/ political dimension in that it subverts "the social, political, economic, and religious *status quo* by transforming the situation of those who are hungry, poor, ill and marginalized."[7] For others, a more proper category is "apocalyptic eschatology." "The agent for the in-breaking of God's kingdom is Jesus, who both proclaims the kingdom and enacts it through miracles and exorcisms." It brings about a reversal of social status, putting down the rich and powerful and exalting the lowly, a theme expressed in the Beatitudes and the Sermon on the Mount.[8]

Finally, the coming of the kingdom demands a personal response. Jesus' preaching includes the call to repentance or, better, conversion, that complete change of mind, heart, and outlook implied by the Greek *metanoia* (Mark 1:15). Parables such as the sower and the seed (Matt 13:1-8), the weeds among the wheat (Matt 13:24-30), the net cast into the sea (Matt 13:47-50), and the sheep and the goats (Matt 25: 31-46) all stress the dimension of personal response. The kingdom of God will come in its fullness when Christ is revealed in glory, vindicating the poor and the righteous, overcoming the power of oppressors, revealing God's justice for all, and binding up the wounds of history.

The Paschal Mystery

The Easter experience of the disciples transformed their understanding of the kingdom that Jesus preached. Like Jesus who had been raised up, they saw themselves called to the fullness of life. Jesus' story became a

6. Brian D. Robinette, *Grammars of Resurrection: A Christian Theology of Presence and Absence* (New York: Crossroad, 2010), 83.

7. Dermot A. Lane, *Keeping Hope Alive: Stirrings in Christian Theology* (New York: Paulist, 1996), 88.

8. Nichols, *Death and Afterlife*, 36.

model for their own, inviting them and us into what has become known as the paschal mystery of his passage from death to life with the Father.

The paschal mystery is a strong motif in Paul's letters. He refers frequently to our participation in Jesus' passage from death to life through his passion and resurrection, a mystery in which his disciples would share; he speaks of considering all he had previously prided himself on as mere rubbish, that he might "know him and the power of his resurrection and [the] sharing of his sufferings by being conformed to his death, if somehow I may attain the resurrection from the dead" (Phil 3:10-11). Baptism initiated this process, uniting us to Christ by baptizing us into his death, so that just as he was raised from the dead, we too might live in newness of life (Rom 6:4; cf. Rom 6:8; 8:17). Thus there is a mystical dimension to our incorporation into the paschal mystery through baptism, something the Catholic funeral rite recalls at the beginning of the service, blessing the body with water symbolic of baptism.

In the Synoptics, entering into the paschal mystery is expressed by the metaphor of taking up our cross just as Jesus did. Jesus says to his disciples, "Whoever wishes to come after me must deny himself, take up his cross, and follow me" (Mark 8:34//Matt 16:24). Luke, always concerned with the practical dimensions of Christian living, adds the word "daily": "If anyone wishes to come after me, he must deny himself and take up his cross daily and follow me" (Luke 9:23). Taking up one's cross implies the willingness to offer one's own life: "For whoever wishes to save his life will lose it, but whoever loses his life for my sake and that of the gospel will save it" (Mark 8:35; cf. Matt 10:39//Luke 9:24).

In John the language is more pastoral, but the idea is the same; the disciple must follow Jesus in what John often calls his glorification: "Amen, amen, I say to you, unless a grain of wheat falls to the ground and dies, it remains just a grain of wheat; but if it dies, it produces much fruit. Whoever loves his life loses it, and whoever hates his life in this world will preserve it for eternal life. Whoever serves me must follow me, and where I am, there also will my servant be" (John 12:24-26). Eternal life is not just a future but a present reality for those who believe in the Son (John 6:40, 54).

Thus, Christian life becomes modeled on that of Jesus and his paschal mystery. Baptism initiates us into the mysteries of Christ's life. We are baptized into his death, share in his sufferings, and are called to take up our crosses after him. But it is particularly in the liturgy of the Eucharist that we are drawn into and experience the saving mysteries of Christ's obedient life, suffering, death, resurrection, and ascension, as Kevin Irwin emphasizes. The *anamnesis* has always been central to the Roman Canon and the structure of the eucharistic prayer, and through the eucharistic prayer and its memorial acclamations we participate or literally "take part in" the paschal mystery.[9]

Vincent Miller calls the paschal mystery the fundamental form of Christian hope. "In it we are strengthened to face and to embrace the suffering and violence of the world."[10] The Second Vatican Council's Pastoral Constitution on the Church in the Modern World saw participation in the paschal mystery as something that was open to all: "For since Christ died for everyone, and since all men are in fact called to one and the same destiny, which is divine, we must hold that the Holy Spirit offers to all the possibility of being partners, in a way known to God, in the paschal mystery" (GS 22).

Thomas Merton gives a powerful expression to what sharing in the paschal mystery of Christ means existentially:

> It is essential to remember that for a Christian "the word of the Cross" is nothing theoretical, but a stark and existential experience of union with Christ in His death in order to share in His resurrection. To fully "hear" and "receive" the word of the Cross means much more than simple assent to the dogmatic proposition that Christ died for our sins. It means to be "nailed to the Cross with Christ," so that the ego-self is no longer the principle of our deepest actions, which now proceeds from Christ living in us. . . . To receive the word of the Cross means the acceptance of a complete self-emptying, a *Kenosis*, in union with the self-emptying of Christ "obedient unto death."[11]

The Church

For all Paul's emphasis in Romans and Galatians that we are saved by faith, not by works of the Law, the communal, ecclesial, and what the later church would call sacramental dimensions of his understanding of God's grace in Christ are clear. His letters are always to or about churches. We are saved by our baptismal incorporation into the one Body of Christ and by being given to drink of the one Spirit (1 Cor 12:12). Paul uses

9. Kevin W. Irwin, "Toward a New Liturgical Movement," *Origins* 40/46 (April 28, 2011): 749.

10. Vincent J. Miller, "Holding On," *America* 204/14 (April 25, 2011): 12.

11. Thomas Merton, *Zen and the Birds of Appetite* (New York: New Directions, 1968), 55–56

these same images, suggestive of baptism and Eucharist, to speak of the ancestors of these largely Jewish Christians to whom he is writing being baptized into Moses in the cloud and the sea of the exodus and drinking from the spiritual rock that is Christ (1 Cor 10:2-4).

Baptism is creative of community by its nature; it breaks down divisions between peoples so that there is no longer Jew or Greek, slave or free, male or female (Gal 3:28; cf. 1 Cor 12:12). The Corinthians become one body, the one Body of Christ, through their participation (*koinōnia*) in his Body and Blood, sharing in the cup of blessing and the bread that is broken (1 Cor 10:16-17). The church itself as a new creation in Christ has a ministry of reconciliation (2 Cor 5:17-18), becoming a sign or instrument of communion with God and of the unity of the entire human race (LG 1). Or as Roger Haight writes, "The church took shape around the originating impulse of God in Jesus toward the kingdom of God in history and finds its raison d'etre in continuing to mediate God's empowerment and supply the social basis for this mission."[12]

The Imitation of Christ

As we saw earlier, the concept of the imitation of Jesus can be traced back as far as Paul, where the eschatological element was predominant. We suffer with Christ in order to be glorified with him (Rom 8:17; cf. 1 Cor 15:49; Phil 3:10-11). In sharing in the cup that has been blessed and the bread that has been broken, we have a communion in his risen life, his Body and Blood (1 Cor 10:16-17). From this perspective, Christ's role as savior and redeemer was much more important than his humanity. The author of 2 Peter wrote that we would "come to share in the divine nature" (2 Pet 1:4). The church fathers continued to develop this eschatological theme: "The idea of the imitation of Christ as essentially a process of divinization or deification was embodied in the works of early theologians in both the East and the West. . . . Though the early church rejected the ancient view that men might become gods during their lifetimes, it fully accepted the idea of deification in the sense of the recovery within man of the image of God and assimilation with God after death."[13]

12. Roger Haight, *Christian Community in History*, vol. 3, *Ecclesial Existence* (New York: Continuum, 2008), 106.

13. Constable, *Three Studies*, 150; see part II, "The Ideal of the Imitation of Christ," 145–217.

In the early church, martyrdom was seen as the preeminent way of imitating Christ, from the idealized picture in Acts of the death of Stephen, the first Christian martyr, who like Jesus dies asking God to forgive his executioners (Acts 7:60), to the way the early martyrs of the church were described. Thus Ignatius of Antioch in his *Letter to the Romans* (ca. 96) prays that he might "be an imitator of the passion of my God,"[14] and the *Letter of the Smyrnaeans* (ca. 156) on the martyrdom of Polycarp describes the martyrs as "disciples and imitators of the Lord."[15] Long after the age of the martyrs had passed from history, they were still being celebrated, but by then their imitation of Christ had been taken up by the monks and nuns who left the cities after the establishment of Christianity for the solitary life in the desert. The early monastic literature speaks often of their efforts to discipline their flesh and struggle against the demons as a new "white" or bloodless martyrdom.

Constable stresses that particularly in the East the imitation of Christ meant placing emphasis on his divinity, moving beyond his human characteristics and becoming one with God as Jesus was. He notes that in Benedict's monastic Rule, Christ is referred to as a man only three times, and the name Jesus is never used: "He is presented as the Lord and God and the life of a monk is one of service and devotion to him as King, Father, Good Shepherd, and Teacher."[16] As the use of the crucifix spread throughout the West in the eighth century, it reflected this emphasis on the divine Jesus; the figure of Christ was often portrayed in the Eastern fashion as alive and triumphant, often clad in royal or priestly vesture. The cross remained a symbol of victory and power as late as the tenth century, though by the eleventh century the figure of the suffering or dead Christ was spreading, even if the wearing of a royal crown was not generally replaced until the thirteenth century.

By the eleventh and twelfth centuries the term *imitatio Christi* took on a new meaning as Christians took an increasing interest in the earthly life of Christ and his humanity, called by Josef Jungmann "the great medieval innovation."[17] The emphasis shifted from his divinity to imitating his human life, reflecting in part a new interest in human behavior as well as a new emphasis on the ethical character of Christianity, par-

---

14. Ignatius of Antioch, *To the Romans* 6, in *The Apostolic Fathers*, trans. J. B. Lightfoot (Grand Rapids, MI: Baker Book House, 1987), 77

15. Ignatius of Antioch, *The Letter of the Smyrnaeans* 17, in Lightfoot, 115.

16. Constable, *Three Studies*, 157.

17. Josef Jungmann, *Pastoral Liturgy* (New York: Herder and Herder, 1962), 56.

ticularly strong in the work of Anselm and Peter Damian. The twelfth-century Cistercians Aelred of Rievaulx, William of St. Thierry, and Bernard of Clairvaux encouraged the use of the imagination in contemplating the humanity of Christ, while Francis of Assisi helped popularize the life of Jesus for ordinary Christians living in the towns and new cities. Ludolpf of Saxony's *Vita Christi*, a work of some two thousand pages, presented meditations on the life of Christ not just for religious but for ordinary lay people; the prologue to the work stresses repeatedly meditating on Christ in order to imitate him.[18] From the fifteenth-century movement known as the *Devotio Moderna* came *The Imitation of Christ*, a work attributed to Thomas à Kempis, perhaps the most popular work after the Bible itself. The author was most probably a member of the Brethren of the Common Life, a community of secular priests and laity founded in the Netherlands by Geert de Groote (1340–84). Monastic in orientation, the *Imitation of Christ* stressed withdrawal into an interior life, struggle, and suffering with Christ.

Along with Ludolph's *Vita Christi*, the *Imitation of Christ* was one of the three books that Ignatius of Loyola had available during his long convalescence, and it shaped the spirituality reflected in his *Spiritual Exercises*, particularly the ideal of following the poor and humble Jesus. It also shaped to a considerable degree the piety of John Calvin. There was an obvious richness in this new Jesus-centered piety, but what was lost was a sense for the *eschaton*, God's kingdom breaking into the lives of God's people, as the emphasis shifted to the *eschata*, the last things—death and judgment, heaven and hell. And influenced by the "acids of modernity," with its scientific and secular ideologies, even the *eschata* were to largely disappear.

Modernity and the Solitary Self

While some find the seeds of modern individualism in the *Devotio Moderna*, it began to flourish with the Reformation. Luther's emphasis on personal faith and his challenge to church authority brought new attention to bear on the individual and the rights of conscience, even if his famous "Here I stand, I can do no other" was more mythological

---

18. For an English translation of the prologue, see Milton Walsh, " 'To Always be Thinking Somehow about Jesus': The Prologue of Ludolph's *Vita Christi*," *Studies in the Spirituality of Jesuits* 43/1 (Spring 2011): 22–39.

than historical. While the medieval person had a strong sense of belonging, both to a community and to a world that was hierarchically ordered, from the Reformation onward the individual increasingly emerged as autonomous, dependent on his or her personal conscience, faith, and point of view.[19] The result was the rise of the solitary self.

The modern "turn toward the subject" can be said to have originated with René Descartes, with his insistence on "a method grounded in the subject's self-presence, a method, in principle, that would prove the same for all thinking, rational persons."[20] The individual emerged as both solitary and supreme, and in subsequent European idealism would become the source of all meaning and value, in contrast to the more objective view of ancient and medieval Western thought. At the same time, as the universe was desacralized or "disenchanted," stripped of the divine presence, it was reduced to a machine, a trend furthered by the development of naturalistic science and by the Enlightenment.

If the twentieth century has seen a culture of individualism flourish in the West, American religion has been particularly marked by it. Salvation is understood individualistically and faith has been privatized. Robert N. Bellah has traced the religious roots of this individualism in his essay "Religion and the Shape of National Culture." So deeply has this individualism shaped our cultural code that he quotes Gilbert Keith Chesterton's remark that "in America, even the Catholics are Protestants."[21]

Bellah argues that the predominant religious tradition in American is sectarian rather than an established church. Those who came to colonial America were for the most part dissenting Protestants, fleeing established churches that had often persecuted them, and so from the beginning they supported religious freedom; as a result, the sacredness of the individual conscience in matters of belief became an absolute. No authority—political, hierarchical, or patriarchal—could compete. In addition, he points to two central Protestant beliefs that strengthened a radical individualism.

First, the Calvinist doctrine of the radical transcendence of God, particularly in the doctrine of predestination, described a God who had

19. The Radical Reformation where the sense of community remained strong may represent an exception.

20. David Tracy, "Theology and the Many Faces of Postmodernity," *Theology Today* 51/1 (1994): 104.

21. Robert N. Bellah, "Religion and the Shape of National Culture," *America* 181/3 (1999): 10.

ordained everything from the beginning, in effect pushing God out of the universe and resulting in a deterministic universe. Into this space, in which God was not needed at all, came an understanding of the self as autonomous. Second, Bellah calls attention to "the near exclusive focus on the relation between Jesus and the individual, where accepting Jesus Christ as one's personal lord and savior becomes almost the whole of piety."[22] Besides contributing to the divinization of the self that represents a modern American version of Gnosticism, it leads to the attitude, "If I'm all right with Jesus, then I don't need the church," an attitude evident in some of the people profiled in his *Habits of the Heart*.

Bellah contrasts this American individualism with its Protestant roots with a Catholic sacramental imagination, shaped particularly by the Eucharist, which tells us who we are as Christians. Though this is difficult for Protestants and even Catholics to understand, he asks, "How can I understand that this bread and this wine is the actual body and blood of Christ and that by participating in the Eucharist I become immediately and physically one with the body of Christ, and so one with the whole of God's creation?"[23] Being a Christian is not primarily about "getting saved." It is about how we have been forgiven, transformed, gentled by God's grace and about how we live in the world. In other words, we are not solitary individuals seeking our salvation in the next life by a personal act of faith but men and women called to community and to service of our brothers and sisters.

We cannot be Christians all by ourselves, nor can we survive as human beings without a network of relations with others, as we are beginning to learn today. The feminist movement in reclaiming the experience of women has put a new emphasis on relationality and interdependence rather than self-sufficiency and autonomy.[24] Those writing on trinitarian theology are stressing the relational nature of the living God. A new sensitivity to ecological and environmental issues has shown us how closely we are dependent on the biosphere that envelops and supports us. Visionary thinkers like Teilhard de Chardin and Thomas Berry see a new global consciousness developing, suggesting that creation itself is

---

22. Ibid., 12.

23. Ibid., 13.

24. See Carol Gilligan, *In a Different Voice: Psychological Theory and Women's Development* (Cambridge, MA: Harvard University Press, 1982); Rosemary Chinnici, *Can Women Re-Imagine the Church?* (New York: Paulist, 1992).

becoming self-conscious.[25] From these movements as well as from new currents in theology, a new, more relational anthropology is emerging.

Retrieving the Kingdom of God

Perhaps the greatest theological challenge to modern religious individualism has been the contemporary retrieval of the biblical notion of the kingdom of God in Christology and, correlatively, the meaning of discipleship. Jesus' message was not primarily about personal salvation, and he said nothing about justification by faith; he proclaimed the coming of the kingdom or reign of God. With this retrieval of the kingdom has come a growing awareness of the social dimensions of the Gospel, particularly in light of the sufferings of so many in our contemporary world. We will consider this new appreciation of the kingdom of God in the works of a number of representative theologians, including Johann Baptist Metz, Jon Sobrino, Elizabeth Johnson, Peter Phan, and Terence Tilley.

Johann Baptist Metz

A Bavarian born in 1928, Metz came of age during the Second World War and was conscripted into the German army at the age of sixteen. After the war he was ordained a priest and did a doctorate in theology. Metz's experience, growing up during the Nazi period, was to profoundly shape his theology, as he sought to come to terms with how German Christians were able "to continue our untroubled believing and praying with our backs to Auschwitz."[26] Though he had begun as a student of Karl Rahner at Innsbruck in the midfifties, he later broke with him, finding his transcendental anthropology too abstract. He also remarked that it was troubling to him that Rahner never mentioned Auschwitz in his theology.[27] His own thought was influenced by Marxist-inspired ideology critiques, by a critique of Enlightenment theology, and by the emergence

25. Pierre Teilhard de Chardin, *The Phenomenon of Man* (New York: Harpers, 1959); Thomas Berry, *The Dream of the Earth* (San Francisco: Sierra Club Books, 1988); Sallie McFague, *The Body of God: An Ecological Theology* (Minneapolis: Fortress, 1993).

26. Johann Baptist Metz, *The Emergent Church* (New York: Crossroad, 1986), 27.

27. According to James Matthew Ashley, *Interruptions: Mysticism, Politics and Theology in the Work of Johann Baptist Metz* (Notre Dame: University of Notre Dame Press, 1988), 123.

of new third-world liberation theologies, particularly after the Medellín Conference of 1968.

Metz begins his critical diagnosis of contemporary Christianity by arguing that Christianity by its very nature is a messianic praxis of discipleship, that is, a discipleship expressed in a preference for those who are underprivileged, a willingness to take sides without hatred or hostility toward others, even to the foolishness of the cross. Yet with the privatization of Christianity that was the result of the Enlightenment, its messianic idea was both interiorized and individualized, and Christianity became little more than a bourgeois religion (*bürgerliche Religion*). Because his theology seeks to reflect on the Christian tradition in the context of world problems and the relation between the kingdom and society, he calls it a "political theology." But he also places considerable emphasis on the mystical.[28]

Central to Metz's thought is what he refers to as the "dangerous memory" of Jesus, the *memoria passionis, mortis et resurrectionis Jesu Christi*, the memory of the passion, death, and resurrection of Jesus, or as he sometimes calls it, "the dangerous memory of freedom."[29] This is what empowers the Christians, calling them to the *imitatio* (*Nachfolge*) *Christi*, the imitation of Christ. Thus Metz specifically reclaims the *imitatio Christi*. In a book written for the superiors of religious communities, Metz stresses that Christology is based on the practice of following Christ, which means that "every Christology is subject to the primacy of practice."[30] In contrast to bourgeois Christianity, "it is only when they imitate Christ that Christians know who it is to whom they have given their consent and who saves them," for "Christological knowledge is not handed down primarily as a concept, but in such stories of the imitation of Christ."[31]

28. Johann Baptist Metz, *Faith in History and Society: Toward a Practical Fundamental Theology*, trans. David Smith (New York: Seabury, 1980), 102; see also Ashley, *Interruptions: Mysticism, Politics and Theology*, 51.

29. Metz, *Faith in History and Society*, 109–11; Bruce T. Morrill notes the influence of Walter Benjamin in Metz's concept of dangerous memory. Morrill, *Anamnesis as Dangerous Memory: Political and Liturgical Theology in Dialogue* (Collegeville, MN: Liturgical Press, 2000), 30n25.

30. Johann Baptist Metz, *Followers of Christ: Perspectives on Religious Life* (New York: Paulist, 1978), 40.

31. Metz, *Faith in History and Society*, 52.

Metz's political theology, which he sees as a practical fundamental theology, places his emphasis not just on eschatology but on an apocalyptic eschatology:

> The faith of Christians is a praxis in history and society that is to be understood as hope in solidarity in the God of Jesus as a God of the living and the dead who calls all men to be subjects in his presence. Christians justify themselves in this essentially apocalyptical praxis (of imitation) in their historical struggle for their fellow men. They stand up for all men in their attempt to become subjects in solidarity with each other. [32]

Metz wants to reclaim the theme of immanent expectation so central to the New Testament. He rejects an evolutionary understanding of time as a rational process without surprises or grace, which in his view has privatized Christian hope, reducing it to the salvation of the individual; such a view is essentially timeless. Instead, he wants to reclaim an apocalyptic vision into which the Messiah can enter. Thus a genuine Christology sees the Christian idea of the imitation of Christ and the apocalyptic idea of immanent expectation as belonging together; it presumes practice, turning toward God in expectation. "It is not possible to imitate Jesus radically, that is, at the level of the roots of life, if 'the time is not shortened.' Jesus' call: 'Follow me!' and the call of Christians: 'Come, Lord Jesus!' are inseparable."[33] Thus a genuine Christology presumes a praxis that can break through those complex social, historical, and psychological conditions that govern history and society, turning toward God in expectation. "What is needed, then, is a praxis of faith in mystical and political imitation."[34]

Bruce Morrill acknowledges that Metz is less clear about how apocalyptic-eschatological narratives motivate solidarity with the living and the dead. He points to just two narratives of suffering that appear in Metz's writings: his reflections on the impact of Auschwitz on contemporary German consciousness and his own personal story of the loss of his companions during the war, a moving story of returning from a night mission to deliver a message, only to find that his entire company had

---

32. Metz, *Faith in History and Society*, 73.
33. Ibid., 172–76 at 176.
34. Ibid., 145.

been wiped out.[35] Metz argues that solidarity with the suffering cannot be sustained without prayer, without that lament or cry to God from the midst of suffering, violence, oppression, and death found so often in the Psalms and in Jesus' cry of abandonment upon the cross.[36] Such prayer is a prayer for Christ's return: "Hence Christianity's oldest prayer is simultaneously the most up-to-date: 'Come Lord Jesus!'" (Rev 22:20)."[37]

Jon Sobrino

Born into a Basque family in Barcelona in 1938, Jon Sobrino went to El Salvador while still a novice in the Society of Jesus. After completing a doctorate in theology (1975) at the Jesuit Hochschule in Frankfurt, Sankt Georgen, he joined the faculty at the University of Central America, the UCA. A member of Ignatio Ellacuría's community when Ellacuría, five of his Jesuit companions, their housekeeper, and her fifteen-year-old daughter were murdered by the Salvadoran military on November 16, 1989, Sobrino escaped death himself as he was in Thailand.

Sobrino has written extensively on Christology. His first major work, *Christology at the Crossroads*, developed a Christology from the perspective of the third world. His approach is similar to that of Metz, who stresses the priority of practice, though like Ignacio Ellacuría who helped shape his thought, Sobrino moves methodologically beyond a narrow focus on the historical Jesus to emphasize what both refer to as the "historical reality" or "historical aspect" of Jesus—that is, "the life of Jesus of Nazareth, his words and actions, his activity and his praxis, his attitudes and his spirit, his fate on the cross (and the resurrection)."[38] In this way Sobrino seeks to incorporate in his Christology both Jesus' "messianic praxis," directed especially to the suffering poor, and his resurrection, without which one is not able to grasp the "whole Christ."[39]

35. Bruce T. Morrill, *Anamnesis as Dangerous Memory*, 44–47; for Metz's story, see his *A Passion for God*, ed. and trans. J. Matthew Ashley (New York: Paulist, 1998), 1–2.

36. Johann Baptist Metz, "The Courage to Pray," in Karl Rahner and Johann Baptist Metz, *The Courage to Pray* (New York: Crossroad, 1981), 12–14.

37. Ibid., 28.

38. Jon Sobrino, *Christ the Liberator: A View from the Victims* (Maryknoll, NY: Orbis, 2001), 50; see Robert LaSalle-Klein, "Jesus of Galilee and the Crucified People: The Contextual Christology of Jon Sobrino and Ignacio Ellacuría" *Theological Studies* 70 (2009): 359.

39. LaSalle-Klein, "Jesus of Galilee and the Crucified People," 362–67.

For Sobrino, the kingdom of God is theology's "most all-embracing theological concept," a kingdom he understands eschatologically; it does not evolve but "breaks in."[40] As with Metz, apocalypticism becomes the horizon for understanding the resurrection, which does not simply anticipate our own resurrection but "looks forward to the vindication of God's justice."[41] The resurrection foreshadows the *eschaton*, God's new age bringing justice to the poor and life to the dead. But this view of history as promise means becoming aware of a mission. Jesus is viewed in terms of the future Parousia, not in terms of his present status as exalted Lord, for "the resurrection sets in motion a life of service designed to implement in reality the eschatological ideals of justice, peace, and human solidarity."[42]

Sobrino develops this theme further in his later works. In *Christ the Liberator* he argues that praxis is the hermeneutical principle for understanding Jesus' resurrection. It is understood as God's victorious work when it generates faith, hope, and action; in other words, it becomes real when others put themselves, often against hope, in the service of the eschatological ideals of justice, peace, solidarity, the life of the weak, community, human dignity, and so on. Thus Sobrino, like Metz, places a priority on practice as the foundational basis for Christology. Borrowing a phrase from Ignacio Ellacuría, he says we need to take the crucified people down from the cross just as God took Jesus down from the cross, expressing in this way the hope that justice will be done to the victims of this world just was it was to the crucified Jesus. As Jesus' liberating actions in his ministry were "signs" and "powers" of the kingdom, pointers generating hope in its possibility, so these partial resurrections generate hope in God's giving life to all the crucified.[43]

Elizabeth Johnson

In her book on Christology, *Consider Jesus*, Fordham's Elizabeth Johnson illustrates how the Jesus of history and his symbol of the reign of God have assumed a central place in Christology. While for centuries Catholic Christology focused on the birth and death of Jesus, with little attention paid to his actual life, a biblically based Christology stresses the importance of his historical ministry and correlates it with what it

---

40. Jon Sobrino, *Christology at the Crossroads* (Maryknoll, NY: Orbis, 1978), 37.
41. Ibid., 243.
42. Ibid., 255.
43. Jon Sobrino, *Christ the Liberator*, 47–49.

means to follow in the way of Jesus today. God's reign means wholeness, healing, and salvation for all. "It is what the scriptures call the situation of *shalom*, peace experienced not only as the absence of war but peace as the fullness of life."[44] Thus the reign of God is a symbol with social and political implications; it is what happens when God's will is really done. She asks her readers to imagine what the reign of God would be like in images taken from urban life in the United States, in Central America, Palestine, or South Africa.

Johnson has the gift of making the abstract practical and concrete. In a marvelous expression, she illustrates how Jesus "enacts" the kingdom. He associated with sinners, offering them forgiveness. He healed the sick, rejecting the widespread belief that their sickness was a punishment for their sins. He drove out demons and healed lepers and others ostracized from the community, bringing them back into life-giving relationships with other human beings. He welcomed them and others, including tax collectors and sinners, into his company to eat and drink with them as a foretaste of the joy of the kingdom in its fullness.[45] The church is the community of believers who seek to imitate the pattern of Jesus' life. To be one of his disciples is "to continue in one's own historical time and place his mission of announcing and signing the coming of the reign of God. . . . Since peace and justice are among the most powerful signs of the reign of God present in this world, it belongs to the essential mission of the church to make these realities more visible in our times, so marked by oppression, violence, injustice, and threat of total destruction."[46] For women especially, it means an end of sexism and their liberation from dominating, patriarchal structures.

Peter Phan

A Vietnamese American theologian, Peter Phan has been particularly concerned to develop a genuinely Asian theology in the context of Asia's religious pluralism. This has raised for him questions about how to be church in Asia, moving from a traditional self-absorption with intraecclesial issues to the conviction that "at the at heart of the Christian faith and practice there lie not the church and all its institutional elements but

---

44. Elizabeth A. Johnson, *Consider Jesus: Waves of Renewal in Christology* (New York: Crossroad, 1990), 52.

45. Ibid., 54–55.

46. Ibid., 77.

the reign of the Triune God."[47] Phan speaks of the evolution of the Asian Catholic churches from their ecclesiocentric or church-centered way of being church, largely the heritage of European colonialism, to a regno-centric or kingdom-centered ecclesiology. He writes,

> In the place of the church the reign of God is now installed as the ultimate goal of all the activities within and without the church. Now both what the church is and what it does are defined by the reign of God and not the other way round. The only reason for the church to exist is to serve the reign of God, that is, to help bring about what has been commonly referred to as the "kingdom values." . . . Every law and policy of the church must pass the litmus test of whether they promote the reign of God.[48]

Thus, the rediscovery of the centrality of the reign of God in the preaching of Jesus has led to a reevaluation of the church's mission. Its "principal goal is no longer 'saving souls' and 'church planting' but bearing witness to the kingdom of God."[49] This is the twofold meaning of conversion for Phan, so prominent in Jesus' teaching. It means, first, becoming a disciple, following after Jesus, doing what he does, and second, proclaiming the approaching kingdom of God. Even the Eucharist, in which we become one with Christ substantially present, should be seen, Phan suggests, as Jesus saying to his disciples that they were to take over his mission and complete it for him. In the context of Asia's religious pluralism, conversion means not adding ex-Buddhists, ex-Hindus, or ex-Muslims to the church, though some may choose to join, but calling all to Christ's mission in the service of the kingdom.[50]

Therefore, witness to the kingdom of God cannot be a one-way proclamation of salvation to "pagans" lacking God's grace. Quoting Pope John Paul's encyclical on mission, which acknowledges that the Spirit is present and active not only in individuals but also in society, history, peoples, cultures, and religions (*Redemptoris Missio* 28), Phan argues that

47. Peter C. Phan, "A Way of Being Church in Asia," *Prism* 20 (Winter 2008): 7.

48. Ibid., 8; see also Thomas Fox, *Pentecost in Asia: A New Way of Being Church* (Maryknoll, NY: Orbis, 2002), 69–77.

49. Peter C. Phan, *In Our Own Tongues: Perspectives from Asia on Mission and Inculturation* (Maryknoll, NY: Orbis, 2003), 40–41; also available as "Proclamation of the Reign of God as Mission of the Church: What for, to Whom, with Whom, and How?"(2001): 5; http://www.sedosmission.org.

50. Ibid., 49–61.

Christian mission must be a search for the presence and activity of the Spirit among the people to be evangelized. Therefore, dialogue emerges as the most effective method of evangelization.

Terrence Tilley

Tilley's work on Christology begins by rejecting the traditional "Christology from above" and "Christology from below" approaches. His book argues that faith is neither merely belief nor merely trust; rather, it means, in his signature expression, "living in and living out the reign of God by engaging in reconciling practices."[51] It was this experience that gave rise to expressions of trust, later formulated as beliefs and inscribed in texts.[52] Like Sobrino, Tilley argues that Christology is properly carried on by engaging in the reconciling practices of the Jesus movement, for soteriology and Christology are inseparable from discipleship. He says that the "reign of God is the reign of human flourishing."[53] Even if the fullness of reconciliation remains in God's hands, to be a disciple means to be at the service of reconciliation, to become agents of reconciliation, allowing others to flourish through reconciling practices that are both political and religious. Ignoring the political aspects of reconciliation would be to deny that reconciliation should permeate all the spaces in which we live.

Much of Tilley's book is an effort to illustrate how the disciples remembered Jesus, not in theory, but in practice; their identity came from what they did and how they lived. This is what constituted the "politics" of the Jesus movement, their remembered practice of exorcising, healing, teaching, and table fellowship. In Tilley's reading, each of these is a reconciling practice. The exorcisms performed by Jesus or those in his movement—however they are to be understood—were a kind of healing that allowed the person to return to his or her circle of family and friends, as in the story of the Gerasene demoniac, which is fundamentally a story of reconciliation (Mark 5:1-20). As Tilley says, "the cures of the Jesus movement removed people from positions of dependence and marginalization. Jesus' curing of lepers, the blind, the hemorrhaging, and others frees them not only from bodily misery but also from the social stigmas that ostracized them."[54]

---

51. Terrence W. Tilley, *The Disciples' Jesus: Christology as Reconciling Practice* (Maryknoll, NY: Orbis, 2008), 252.

52. Ibid., 24.

53. Ibid., 244.

54. Ibid., 145–46.

Similarly, Jesus' teaching, captured in his aphorisms and parables, was not primarily about God's nature, or heaven, or a religious organization, but about how to live, how to relate to each other and to God. Consider the story of the man who was robbed and left bleeding on the road (Luke 10:25-37). Tilley argues that while the gospels do not report the disciples forgiving sins, "the practice of the Jesus-movement is the mutual, free forgiveness of all that stands in the way of reconciliation."[55] So too the table fellowship practiced by the Jesus movement, a banquet that welcomed the stranger, the Other, and the opponent, showed how a renewed and reconciled community could live and eat together.

Even the Last Supper in Tilley's reading of the texts is less a gathering of just the Twelve than an inclusive gathering of disciples, women among them; thus it is an example of inclusive table fellowship and hospitality as a reconciling practice of Jesus and his disciples.[56] The hospitality of the Jesus movement suggests not proselytism but a mission *inter gentes* rather than *ad gentes*. His conclusion is that practice, not theory, is at the heart of Christian life; demanding theological or ideological conformity in a situation of diversity is not a reconciling practice. The Christian mission is neither Christocentric nor ecclesiocentric, but theocentric.[57]

Contemporary Expressions of the Kingdom of God

The resurrection of Jesus transformed the disciples' understanding of the kingdom of God. At times Paul describes it as a present reality: "the kingdom of God is not a matter of food and drink, but of righteousness, peace, and joy in the holy Spirit" (Rom 14:17). But most often he puts the emphasis on the eschatological future, stressing that the immoral and unjust will not inherit the kingdom (1 Cor 6:9-10; Gal 5:21). John refers to the kingdom only twice, and then in the context of transformation by the Spirit (John 3:3, 5). Most often he uses the term "eternal life" to express salvation in Jesus, and again it has both a present and a future dimension (John 6:54).

The fact that both Paul and John associate the kingdom of God with the Spirit should not be overlooked, for the Spirit of Jesus, the Holy Spirit, is present wherever men and women are reaching out in compassionate

55. Ibid., 170.
56. Ibid., 184.
57. Ibid., 260.

service toward others, bringing justice for the poor and the oppressed, setting people free, witnessing to reconciliation and peace. Too often in Western theology the work of the Spirit is ignored. Christians by their baptism are incorporated into the life of the Trinity; they become part of the people of God, disciples of Jesus, a community gathered in the Spirit. Our communion (*koinōnia*) in the divine life is transformative.

Every generation of Christians needs to translate Jesus' metaphor of the kingdom or reign of God into language that makes sense to the people of the time. At times the kingdom has been reduced to the life of the blessed in heaven or narrowly identified with the church. The Second Vatican Council (1962–65) taught that the church receives the mission to proclaim and establish the kingdom among all peoples, while the church itself represents its initial budding forth on earth (LG 5). We find the kingdom emerging where people are living the Beatitudes, in the stories of contemporary martyrs for justice and reconciliation, in the struggle for the recognition and inclusion of the marginalized, and in particular in efforts to secure the rights of the most vulnerable, including the unborn. The power of the kingdom, the initial realization of God's reign is the Spirit, incorporating us into love of the Father and the Son. The kingdom will find its completion when Christ returns to gather his own, and God will be all in all.

Many contemporary theologians stress the role of Jesus' disciples to unleash or "enact" the power of the kingdom through recalling the dangerous memory of Jesus' death and resurrection, ministering to the victims of injustice, or engaging in reconciling practices, as we have seen. For Albert Nolan, the kingdom of God is a kingdom of love and service, a kingdom of human brotherhood in which each person is loved and respected. Because God has revealed himself as a God of compassion, we come to believe in and hope for such a kingdom through acting with compassion toward others ourselves. For it is precisely human compassion that releases God's power in the world, the only power that can bring about the miracle of the kingdom.[58]

Michael Cook sees the kingdom as "Jesus' comprehensive term for the blessings of salvation insofar as it denotes the divine activity at the center of all human life." In other words, God is not far from us. At the same time, faith "is Jesus' human, experiential term for salvation itself insofar as it denotes the human response, universally valid, of openness,

---

58. Albert Nolan, *Jesus Before Christianity* (Maryknoll, NY: Orbis, 1978), 84.

acceptance, and commitment." Jesus' disciples are called into a special relationship with him so that they might become an extension of him (a "body") in the world.[59]

Writing from a feminist perspective, Elisabeth Schüssler Fiorenza sees the *basileia* (kingdom) of God as experienced in the healing activity of Jesus. His "*basileia* vision makes people whole, healthy, cleansed and strong. It restores people's humanity and life." It is being realized wherever people are liberated from oppressive power structures and dehumanizing power systems.[60]

Pope Benedict's approach is decidedly different. He sees the new proximity of the kingdom, the distinguishing feature of Jesus' message, as being found in Jesus himself. "Through Jesus' presence and action, God has here and now entered actively into history in a wholly new way. The reason why *now* is the fullness of time (Mk 1:15), why *now* is in a unique sense the time of conversion and penance, as well as the time of joy, is that in Jesus it is God who draws near to us."[61] In his view, regnocentrism, making the kingdom the center of Jesus' message to harness humankind's energies toward the world's future, a world governed by peace, justice, and the conservation of the creation, amounts to a secular-utopian idea of the kingdom. It means that the establishment of the kingdom becomes a common task, makes the missionary evangelization of other religions unnecessary, and pushes God offstage. He is no longer needed.[62]

Conclusion

The way of Jesus has been differently expressed in Christian history. Jesus called men and women into a new family of those who do the will of God. He chose them to follow after him as his disciples, proclaiming the reign of God. As early as Paul, Christians were being called to imitate Christ by participating in his paschal mystery, by being incorporated into his death so as to share in his resurrection. The Synoptics challenged the early Christians to take up their own crosses and come after Jesus;

59. Michael L. Cook, *The Jesus of Faith* (New York: Paulist, 1981), 56–57.
60. Elisabeth Schüssler Fiorenza, *In Memory of Her: A Feminist Reconstruction of Christian Origins* (New York: Crossroad, 1985), 123.
61. Pope Benedict XVI, *Jesus of Nazareth* (New York: Doubleday, 2007), 60.
62. Ibid., 53–55.

John reminded them that the seed must die if it was to bring forth fruit, stressing that Jesus was "the way and the truth and the life" (John 14:6). The earliest name for the disciples seems to have been "the Way." It would not have occurred to the early Christians that they were to challenge the oppressive structures of the Roman Empire, such as slavery, though for the baptized, social relations were to be transformed in light of their new life in Christ. Paul's letter to Philemon, sending back the runaway slave Onesimus, is an example of this.

In the age of persecution, martyrdom was seen as the preeminent way of imitating Christ. When the church became officially established, many sought a new kind of "white" martyrdom in the monastic life. But the Christ imitated was the divine Christ who triumphed over sin and death and who, enthroned at God's right hand, promised a new heaven and a new earth.

In the early second millennium a new interest in the humanity of Jesus became evident in Christian spirituality and art. It was reflected in the *Imitation of Christ*, the *Spiritual Exercises* of Saint Ignatius, and the piety of John Calvin. But with the late Middle Ages and the Reformation's concern with the doctrine of the redemption, the sense for the coming *eschaton* shifted to a concern for the *eschata*—death and judgment, heaven and hell. This new awareness of the individual was only to increase with modernity, while modernity's increasingly secular and empirical biases made even the *eschata* a matter of personal belief.

The religious individualism of Western, particularly American, Christianity was challenged by developments in Christology, particularly the rediscovery of Jesus' emphasis on the kingdom of God and his call to a costly discipleship. We saw how this rediscovery of the kingdom influenced the works of representative theologians such as Johann Baptist Metz, Jon Sobrino, Elizabeth Johnson, Peter Phan, and Terrence Tilley. Common to them all is a strong sense for the primacy of practice.

Metz stresses the *imitatio Christi*, recovering the messianic praxis of discipleship. For Sobrino, it means focusing on the "historical reality" of Jesus, his activity and practice, which in contemporary terms means taking the crucified of the world down from the cross. For Elizabeth Johnson, discipleship means making visible in our times, so marked by oppression and violence, the signs of the coming reign of God. For Peter Phan, writing in the context of the church in Asia, it means moving from an ecclesiocentric to a regnocentric ecclesiology, calling all, both Christians and those of other religious traditions, to Christ's mission in the service of the kingdom. Finally, for Terrence Tilley, it means living in and living out the reign of God by engaging in reconciling practices, both personal and religious. Thus, a new appreciation of the reign of God has stressed the importance of practice, resulting in new political or liberation theologies, a new understanding of the church and its mission, and a new openness of religious pluralism. The coming of the kingdom in its fullness will mean overcoming the powers of death; it will bring justice, reconciliation, peace, and the renewal of creation.

Pope Benedict XVI remains a dissenting voice. He views regnocentric theologies as based on a secular-utopian idea of the kingdom, making evangelization of non-Christians unimportant and acting as though God were no longer necessary for the realization of the kingdom.

4

The Mystery of the Resurrection

The church began with the resurrection and the gift of the Spirit. Scattered by the trauma of the crucifixion, the disciples reassembled, drawn by their Easter experience of Jesus risen and triumphant. The report of the first witnesses spread quickly: "The Lord has truly been raised and has appeared to Simon" (Luke 24:34). From the New Testament accounts, we know that they were slow to recognize him and hesitant to believe, and yet they were transformed by their experience. But what their experience was or how the risen Jesus manifested himself to them is difficult, if not impossible, to reconstruct.

In Mark, the women at the tomb on Sunday morning are told to tell the disciples and Peter, "he is going before you to Galilee; there you will see him, as he told you" (Mark 16:7), suggesting that the appearances took place in Galilee. Matthew follows Mark but adds an appearance to Mary Magdalene and the women in Jerusalem (Matt 28:9-10), reflecting another ancient tradition that Mary Magdalene was the first witness to the resurrection.[1] Luke, most probably for theological reasons, transfers the appearances to Jerusalem and its environs. John preserves several traditions, a first appearance to Mary Magdalene (John 20:11-17), several appearances to the disciples in Jerusalem (John 20:19-29), and in the Johannine appendix (John 21), an appearance to seven disciples in Galilee.

---

1. See Gerald O'Collins and Daniel Kendall, "Mary Magdalene as Major Witness to Jesus' Resurrection," *Theological Studies* 48/4 (1987): 645. They conclude that women were the first or among the first witnesses, with Mary having a lead role.

In light of our eschatological concern and keeping in mind James Alison's comment on the "density of the resurrection,"[2] we will focus in this chapter on the resurrection. We will look at two distinct expressions of the Easter tradition. Then we will ask, what do we understand by the risen body, does the resurrection for the faithful take place immediately after death or is there an intermediate state, and how do we imagine the nature of our eschatological hope? Finally, we will consider an emerging conviction that the resurrection is not just something that each of us looks forward to personally; it also has a social dimension.

The Resurrection

While the resurrection of Jesus is presupposed throughout the New Testament, there are two distinct strands of the Easter tradition: the earlier Easter kerygma or proclamation and the later Easter stories.[3] The Easter kerygma—short, formulaic proclamations of the resurrection—predates the gospels and even Paul, whose letters are the first New Testament documents. Paul cites a very early example in his First Letter to the Corinthians, which besides listing the witnesses is evidence that Paul himself was instructed in the Easter tradition:

> For I handed on to you as of first importance what I also received: that Christ died for our sins in accordance with the scriptures; that he was buried; that he was raised on the third day in accordance with the scriptures; that he appeared to Cephas [Peter], then to the Twelve. After that, he appeared to more than five hundred brothers at once, most of whom are still living, though some have fallen asleep. After that he appeared to James, then to all the apostles. (1 Cor 15:3-7)

Originating in early Christian preaching or liturgy, these examples of the Easter kerygma are neither dramatic nor detailed; they state the belief of the early Christian communities that Jesus has been raised and that

2. James Alison, *Raising Abel: The Recovery of the Eschatological Imagination* (New York: Crossroad, 1996), 28.

3. Walter Kasper, *Jesus the Christ* (New York: Paulist, 1976), 125–26; see also Dermot A. Lane, *Keeping Hope Alive: Stirrings in Christian Theology* (New York: Paulist, 1996), 12–13.

there are witnesses (Acts 2:32-33, 36; 3:20; 5:30-31; Rom 1:3-4; 10:9; Luke 24:34). While the disciples' Easter experience was unique, "the truth of the experience, the *that* of Jesus' resurrection, was mediated by a process of formulaic condensation."[4] Romans 10:9 still sounds like a confessional formula: "if you confess with your mouth that Jesus is Lord and believe in your heart that God raised him from the dead, you will be saved." Similar testimonies appear in what were early hymns (e.g., 1 Tim 3:16), some of which were clearly pre-Pauline (Phil 2:6-11).

The Easter stories are quite different; they are dramatic narrative accounts complete with dialogue and detail about persons, places, and circumstances. They can be divided into two different types: stories of the discovery of the empty tomb and stories of the appearances. They developed later in the tradition; note that Mark, the first gospel, has an empty tomb story but no appearance stories, excluding the material in the later Markan appendices (Mark 16:9-20). The message of the young man at the tomb that "He is going before you to Galilee" (Mark 15:7) suggests that it was in Galilee that Jesus appeared to the disciples, as we saw earlier.

Rather than being historical or reportorial narratives, the Easter stories are theological constructions to help later generations of Christians come to Easter faith. Their lessons are as relevant to us today as they were to the early Christians. The empty tomb stories remind us that "it was the whole Jesus, body and soul, that was raised up, thereby countering any reduction of the resurrection to a purely spiritual or merely mystical experience."[5] The Easter appearance stories teach us that one does not have to see the risen Jesus to believe (John 20:29), that he is encountered "in the breaking of the bread," the community's Eucharist (Luke 24:35; cf. John 21:12-23), that the disciples have been missioned to preach, baptize, and pastor in Jesus' name (Matt 28:19; Luke 24:47-48; John 20:21-23; 21:15-17). Many commentators consider the story of Paul's vision of the risen Jesus and conversion in the Acts of the Apostles as another Easter story (Acts 9:1-8; 22:3-16; 26:12-18).

While the resurrection of Jesus cannot be proved, the New Testament is careful to list the witnesses, and there is the evidence of the story of the empty tomb. In some passages Peter appears as the first witness (1 Cor 15:5; Luke 24:34), while others list Mary Magdalene (Matt 28:9-10;

---

4. Ben F. Meyer, *Christus Faber: The Master Builder and the House of God* (Allison Park, PA: Pickwick Publications, 1992), 140.

5. Lane, *Keeping Hope Alive*, 103.

John 20:11-17). Then there is Paul himself, whose testimony is the earliest and is important because he initially persecuted those first followers of Jesus who claimed that he had been raised up. Terence Nichols makes some important points about the witnesses. He argues that Paul is probably the best witness because of his initial hostility and the fact that some of the witnesses he lists in 1 Corinthians 15: 3-8 were still alive at the time he was writing and could have easily challenged his account. The fact that some of the witnesses were women is also significant, as the testimony of women was not highly regarded in the patriarchal culture of the day; it took the testimony of two women to equal the testimony of one man.[6] Therefore, from a critical perspective, listing women among the witnesses is not the strongest argument. They must have been named because their testimony was true.

If indeed the tomb had not been empty, that story could easily have been contradicted by others. While the story is not conclusive evidence, the fact that the story of the apostles stealing his body is mentioned by Matthew suggests that such a story was indeed making the rounds in Jerusalem, which in turn suggests the need to explain the empty tomb (Matt 28:11-15). Indeed, the tradition that the tomb was empty is older than the gospel narratives themselves. Walter Kasper argues that the story was not an account of the empty tomb's discovery but is best explained as a cultic narrative used by the Jerusalem Christian community to honor the tomb of Jesus. However, its cultic nature does not imply that there is no history behind the tradition; if the tomb had not been empty, a tradition celebrating it would have made no sense.[7]

Understanding the Resurrection

How should we understand the resurrection? Of course there are some who will always remain skeptical, arguing on the basis of a naïve scientism or rationalism that the dead cannot rise. One positive approach, taken by Nichols, is integrative. It challenges a naturalism that narrows reality to our three-dimensional, spatio-temporal world. Appealing to the work of physicists today, Nichols seeks to expand our vision of "na-

6. Terence Nichols, *Death and Afterlife: A Theological Introduction* (Grand Rapids, MI: Brazos Press, 2010), 141–42.

7. Kasper, *Jesus the Christ*, 127–28; Gerald O'Collins gives an impressive list of scholars who hold the essential reliability of the empty tomb story; *Jesus Risen: An Historical, Fundamental, and Systematic Examination of Christ's Resurrection* (New York: Paulist, 1987), 123.

ture" to a more comprehensive view open to different universes, one which might leave room for a vision of Jesus' bodily existence in a state different from ours. Such a transformed state would not take place through nature *unaided*, but by a "supernaturalized nature" transformed by grace. He draws an analogy between the resurrection and a contemporary approach to healing miracles that integrates the body's natural healing powers with grace, so that the so-called laws of nature are not violated but elevated or empowered.[8]

Another approach asks what kind of an event the resurrection of Jesus was. For scholars such as Rudolf Bultmann, Christ is risen in the kerygma, for "he meets us in the word of preaching and nowhere else,"[9] while for Willi Marxsen, the resurrection means that the "cause" of Jesus goes on, calling on the disciples to put themselves, like Jesus, totally at the service of their neighbors, a faith found by Peter after the death of Jesus.[10] For these scholars, the resurrection is reduced to a subjective event in the lives of the disciples; it is no longer something that happened to Jesus.

On the other hand, an overly objective approach turns the resurrection into a this-worldly event, perceptible by any neutral observer. To counter this, some theologians say that the resurrection was not a historical event. This does not mean that it did not happen but that it is not the kind of event subject, at least potentially, to the canons of empirical verification. Even if there had been cameras at the tomb, there would not have been "film at eleven"! The risen Jesus disclosed himself in some mysterious way to the disciples, but they did not witness the resurrection itself. Kasper acknowledges that the resurrection had a historical dimension in that it happened to the crucified Jesus of Nazareth.[11] The resurrection thus has touched history but cannot be proved; what remains is the testimony of the witnesses and Christianity itself.

Theologically, it makes far more sense to see the resurrection neither as a subjective event, an interior feeling on the part of the disciples, nor as an objective event in the world accessible to any neutral observer. Nevertheless, it was a real event, and it happened to Jesus. The Easter stories suggest that there is something very different about the risen

8. Nichols, *Death and Afterlife*, 143–44.

9. Rudolf Bultmann, *Kerygma and Myth*, vol. 1 (London: SPCK, 1953), 41.

10. Willi Marxsen, *The Resurrection of Jesus of Nazareth* (Philadelphia: Fortress, 1970), 125–26.

11. Kasper, *Jesus the Christ*, 150.

Jesus' mode of existence. He comes and goes at will, passing through walls and locked doors, appearing in different places. The disciples do not recognize him; they react with fear, uncertainty, and nonrecognition; they think they are seeing a ghost; they have to be led to faith. In other words, there is something nonobjectifiable about the risen Jesus as he is experienced by the disciples.

But the fact that the risen Jesus did not appear to his enemies, to those who had closed their hearts to him and to his message, is very suggestive. Seeing the risen Jesus required receptivity on the part of those who became witnesses to his risen presence, a prior relationship based on openness and love. In the words of Dermot Lane, "those who had followed Jesus in faith now come to recognize him in a different way as risen in light of their transforming experience of his new, real, personal presence."[12] Even though he seems the exception to the rule just mentioned, Paul's case was similar. Paul was a deeply religious man, seeking God's righteousness, no matter how hostile he was toward the first disciples of Jesus; thus he saw God's revelation of Christ to him as a call and grace (Gal 1:15-16). Roger Haight speaks of the "transcendent character" of the resurrection: "It is known as a revelatory religious experience and not in an empirical, historical perception or an objective inference from such an event."[13] In recounting his own experience Paul uses the word "revelation" (*apocalypsis*) to describe his encounter with the risen Jesus (Gal 1:12), though N. T. Wright insists that Paul refers in this and other passages (1 Cor 9:1; 15:8-11) "to the moment when he met and saw Jesus."[14] Reacting against post-Enlightenment rationalism, Wright may overstate the case. Raymond Brown is more measured; he argues that the eschatological nature of the resurrection means that "the categories of space and time, the categories of ordinary human experience such as 'seeing' and 'speaking' supply us with a language that is only analogous and approximate when we use it to describe the eschatological."[15]

From a theological perspective, the resurrection of Jesus is a properly eschatological event, one that happens on the other side of death. It means that God's future has entered into time and history; it means that

---

12. Dermot A. Lane, *The Reality of Jesus* (New York: Paulist, 1975), 61.

13. Roger Haight, *Jesus Symbol of God* (Maryknoll, New York: Orbis, 1999), 144.

14. N. T. Wright, *The Resurrection of the Son of God* (Minneapolis: Fortress, 2003), 378.

15. Raymond E. Brown, *The Virginal Conception and the Bodily Resurrection of Jesus* (New York: Paulist, 1973), 125.

the end of time has arrived, that the *eschaton* is already present. Jesus lives now in God's presence, but because he is still one of us, he can be present in our spatio-temporal world, though in a different way than during his historical ministry. He is present in and through the Spirit; he is present in the Eucharist, in his body the church, and in memory and hope.

Finally, the resurrection reveals God's vindication of Jesus and his ministry. God has not forgotten the just one, has not abandoned him to Sheol, but has raised him to life. The resurrection shows that God's love is stronger than death. The resurrection of Jesus reveals the destiny of those who die in communion with God; it is a sign of God's solidarity with all the victims of history. They also will not be forgotten.

The Risen Body

If Christian belief in the resurrection of the body meets with skepticism today, St. Paul experienced a similar problem with some of the members of the Corinthian church. The questions they raised seem surprisingly contemporary: How are the dead raised? What kind of bodies will they have? What is a spiritual body?

His instruction in 1 Corinthians 15 begins by rooting Christian faith and hope in the resurrection of Jesus, though his appeal reaches beyond the event of Easter to the belief of the general resurrection of the dead current among some groups in the Judaism of his day. "If there is no resurrection of the dead, then neither has Christ been raised. And if Christ has not been raised, then empty [too] is our preaching; empty, too, your faith. . . . For if the dead are not raised, neither has Christ been raised, and if Christ has not been raised, your faith is vain; you are still in your sins" (1 Cor 15:14-17)

Then he develops his theology of Christ, the last Adam. Since Christ has indeed been raised, he is the "firstfruits" of those who have fallen asleep: "For just as in Adam all die, so too in Christ shall all be brought to life, but each one in proper order: Christ the firstfruits; then, at his coming, those who belong to Christ; then comes the end, when he hands over the kingdom to his God and Father, when he has destroyed every sovereignty and every authority and every power" (1 Cor 15:22-24).

But Paul's language becomes less clear when he tries to answer the question of what kind of body the dead will have when they have been raised. He turns to analogies for what is intelligible but not easily imagined, using as the root metaphor the seed or kernel that is sown in the earth to grow up as a sheaf of wheat. The idea here is of radical change within continuity, leading to a very different "body" from the seed buried in the earth. Early in this letter he argues for sexual restraint because of the continuity between the earthly body and the heavenly one (1 Cor 6:13-18), with the implication that a body dominated by sin cannot inherit the kingdom of God (1 Cor 6:9-10). At the same time, Paul's view, based on what we have called the nonobjectifiable character of the risen Jesus as he manifested himself to his disciples, was very different from the Jewish view of the time, which identified the risen body completely with the earthly body and "the world of the resurrection simply a continuation of the world of the present."[16]

In 1 Corinthians 15 Paul argues that not all flesh (*sarx*) is the same, distinguishing between human beings and the various animals. Then he notes that different kinds of bodies have different characteristics; there are earthly bodies and there are heavenly bodies like the sun, the moon, and the stars. Just as these bodies differ, so also in the resurrection of the dead, with the corruptible and dishonorable being raised as incorruptible and glorious, a natural body (*sōma psychikon*) is now raised as a spiritual body (*sōma pneumatikón*). While some commentators draw a distinction between flesh (*sarx*) and body (*sōma*) in Paul's usage—holding that Paul means that the risen body will be without its corruptible aspects, those carnal, sexual, and fleshy aspects associated with *sarx*—Robinette cites other scholars to argue against this. In this view, which includes his own, the expression "flesh and blood" (1 Cor 15:50) and a parallel passage that speaks of "the unjust" not entering the kingdom of heaven (1 Cor 6:9-11) are two examples of a Semitic usage "referring to the whole human being, most usually in contexts emphasizing creatureliness, weakness, and, in this particular case, alienation from God due to sin."[17] Both passages indicate that our bodily conduct matters because it is our bodies that will be raised.

But what is the meaning of a spiritual body? It seems like a contradiction in terms, an oxymoron. It does not mean a body made up of spirit, as that would no longer be a body. As Brian Robinette says, "resurrection is not decreation or dematerialization, but material creation most fully

---

16. Joseph Ratzinger, *Eschatology: Death and Eternal Life*, 2nd ed., trans. Michael Waldstein (Washington, DC: Catholic University of America Press, 1988), 169.

17. Brian D. Robinette, *Grammars of Resurrection: A Christian Theology of Presence and Absence* (New York: Crossroad, 2009), 155.

realized."[18] Paul's contrast is between an earthly body animated by a soul (psychē), a natural principle, and a human body now completely animated and transformed by the risen Jesus, the last Adam who has become a "life-giving spirit" (1 Cor 15:45). One is earthly, subjected to the constraints of our spatio-temporal existence, the other, reflecting the glorified state of the risen Jesus, is a bodily existence beyond the possibilities of our natural world that we can neither objectify nor imagine (cf. Phil 3:21).

Caroline Walker Bynum gives ample evidence of how speculation about the constitution of the risen body continued to fascinate artists, philosophers, and theologians. For many of the church fathers, material continuity was important. Irenaeus (d. ca. 202) and Tertullian (d. ca. 220) stressed a materialist understanding of the resurrection, the reassembling of the particles of our flesh by God at the end of time so that nothing was lost, "neither genitals, nor intestines, nor eyelashes, nor toes."[19] Continuity was found in the body's materiality. Thus Tertullian spoke of the resurrection as the reassembling of "bits," with our organs being preserved, while defects are healed and mutilations undone so that we rise whole. Gregory of Nyssa (ca. 394) held a similar view, though his position was not always consistent; he taught that the body would rise without age or sex. Jerome (ca. 347–420) also held to the metaphor of reassembling, comparing it to the restoring of a ship after shipwreck; but he insisted we would be raised with our genitals, so that there would be gender inequality and social hierarchy in heaven, a view very similar to that of Augustine (354–430), who also argued that men would have beards because beauty was a property of the risen body.[20]

Origen (ca. 185–254) seems to have taken a different approach, though we no longer have his treatise on the resurrection, and some of his writings were revised in a more orthodox direction in their Latin versions. He taught that we would have a spiritual, luminous body in heaven, without its bodily functions, but its continuity would be through the form (*eidos*) that constitutes the body rather than through some material substratum, for the body itself is in a state of flux in this life and changes

18. Ibid., 158.

19. Caroline Walker Bynum, *The Resurrection of the Body in Western Christianity, 200–1336* (New York: Columbia University Press, 1995), 59.

20. Ibid., 35–103; the reference to Jerome's theory of gender inequality and social hierarchy in heaven is from Elizabeth Clark's review of Peter Brown's *Body and Society*, in *Journal of Religion* 70 (1990): 432–36.

after death. The form safeguarded identity between this life and the next.[21]

The Middle Ages

How the body was to be reconstituted continued to be a subject of fascination. Artists often represented the martyrs carrying the parts of their bodies severed from them in torture or death; they showed the saints rising from their tombs or being regurgitated by the animals or fish that had devoured them. The scholastics continued to speculate along the lines of Augustine on the reassembling of the body. In his *Sentences* Peter Lombard (ca. 1100–1160) pondered the age, height, and sex of those raised, whether they would have fingernails and hair, and how the bodies of those in hell could burn without being consumed. John Scotus Eriugena (ca. 815–ca. 877), whose thought was more influenced by the Greek East than the Latin West, offered an alternative closer to the thought of Origen. He saw the body not as a collection of particles but as an underlying pattern, like Origen's *eidos*. Using Paul's image of the seed, he stressed transformation rather than reassembling and argued that just as Christ rose without biological sex, so would we. Hildegard of Bingen (1098–1179), though she wrote little about the end times, followed Peter Lombard's approach, a covering of the bones of the dead with flesh, but only through the grace of God, without which the body would tend only toward corruption and fragmentation. The Cistercians spoke of a double resurrection, first of the soul, revivified in the church through the Word of God, and then the resurrection of the body at the end of time.[22]

Thomas Aquinas

Thomas Aquinas (1225–74), in his commentary on 1 Corinthians 15 (preserved in the notes of one of his disciples), rejected Paul's analogy of the seed lest it imply that the resurrection is a natural phenomenon, the unfolding of a preordained pattern within the organism rather than a supernatural work of grace.[23] Adapting Aristotle's hylomorphism, he argued that the soul, the *anima forma corporis*, is the spiritual "form" of the body, though his notion of "form" or "soul" went beyond that of Aristotle. While Aristotle's form could not subsist without matter, Aqui-

21. Ibid., 64–67.
22. Ibid., 121–69; Bynum offers examples from medieval art of these imaginative renderings of the resurrection following pages 114.
23. Ibid., 232–34.

nas held that the soul is both the form of the body and a subsisting im-mortal spirit and therefore able to subsist without the body. Ratzinger calls this a complete transformation of Aristotelianism; the spirit, because it does not belong to this world, is neither individual nor personal. But the spirit joined to the body, precisely as spirit, makes us persons open to immortality.[24]

However, because it is ordered toward matter, the soul apart from the body is incomplete. Aquinas goes so far as to say that the soul apart from the body is not a person. Bynum quotes Aquinas as saying that until the resurrection, " 'I' am not truly 'I,' " or as he says in the *Summa Theologiae*, "the soul is no more the person than a hand or foot is the person."[25] Thomas himself was never really able to explain how the soul apart from the body was able to understand individual things, suggesting that per-haps God infused the species or ideas necessary for consciousness.[26]

Resurrection Immediately after Death?

This incompleteness of the soul apart from the body, along with the problematic aspects of its self-identity, has led some in modern times to the view that the resurrection for the just takes place at the moment of death. Often referred to as "resurrection in death," it represents an effort to move beyond imaginative thinking about the end times by arguing that the *eschaton* is by definition beyond time. It represents God's future, no longer subject to spatio-temporal—thus material—categories, for eternity is by definition timeless. Against those who argue for an inter-mediate state between death and the general resurrection, they argue that the *eschaton* begins with the moment of death, so that those who have been faithful share fully in the resurrection of Jesus. Rahner, for example, points out that the doctrine of the intermediate state is only a doctrine, not a dogma, and so remains open to discussion by theologians.[27]

Other Catholic theologians reject this view that the resurrection of the body and general judgment take place at death, as does the official

24. Ratzinger, *Eschatology*, 148–49.

25. Bynum, *The Resurrection of the Body*, 257; she is citing Thomas Aquinas, *In I Cor.* chap. 15, lectio 2, and *Summa Theologiae* I, q. 75, a. 4, reply obj. 2.

26. ST I, 89, 4.

27. For example, Karl Rahner, "The Intermediate State," in *Theological Investiga-tions*, vol. 17 (New York: Crossroad, 1981), 114–15.

church. In 1979 the Congregation for the Doctrine of the Faith published a letter reaffirming the traditional view on an "intermediate state":

> The Church affirms that a spiritual element survives and subsists after death, an element endowed with consciousness and will, so that the "human self" subsists. To designate this element, the Church uses the word "soul," the accepted term in the usage of Scripture and Tradition. Although not unaware that this term has various meanings in the Bible, the Church thinks that there is no valid reason for rejecting it; moreover, she considers that the use of some word as a vehicle is absolutely indispensable in order to support the faith of Christians.[28]

For Ratzinger, the idea of resurrection in death is neither logical nor firmly rooted in Scripture. First, while it solves the problem of eschatological fulfillment for the individual, it overlooks the fulfillment of the historical process itself, which is a significant aspect of Christian hope. Second, from a biblical perspective, he argues that the early Christians shared the faith of the Judaism of their day about the dead continuing to live as souls or spirits prior to the final judgment, though the early Christians saw this from a Christological perspective. Marshaling a host of apocryphal and biblical texts, he appeals to Enoch 22, with its picture of the just gathered around a life-giving spring, separated from the unjust; to 4 Ezra, where the pains of the unjust have already begun even before the final judgment, while the martyrs have been received into Abraham's bosom; to Paul, who refers several times to the dead who live in Christ (1 Thess 4:16; 5:10; Phil 1:23; cf. 2 Cor 5:1-10); to Luke's reference to Lazarus in Abraham's bosom and Dives in hell (Luke 16:19-31); and to the Good Thief, who will be "with me in Paradise" (Luke 23:43).[29] According to Ratzinger, the "intermediate state" between death and the resurrection was to receive its systematic formulation in the high Middle Ages with the teaching on the immortality of the soul.[30]

28. Congregation for the Doctrine of the Faith, Letter on Certain Questions Concerning Eschatology (May 17, 1979); this view was amplified in the International Theological Commission's 1992 document Some Current Questions in Eschatology, *Irish Theological Quarterly*, 58 (1992): 209–39; for an extended discussion on the intermediate state, see the U.S. Lutheran–Roman Catholic Dialogue, "The Hope of Eternal Life" (2010), 6–16.

29. Peter Phan sees Ratzinger's evaluation of the resurrection in death hypothesis "as excessively sweeping and laboring under non sequiturs." See his "Contemporary Context and Issues in Eschatology," *Theological Studies* 55 (1994): 527.

30. Ratzinger, *Eschatology*, 119; see also Rahner, "The Intermediate State," 119–22.

Brian Robinette holds that the proper understanding of the relationship between individual and general eschatology requires an acknowledgment of an "intermediate state" between individual death and the general resurrection."[31] Similarly, Terence Nichols maintains that the theory of an immediate resurrection finds little support in either Scripture or tradition. He notes that even Jesus was not immediately resurrected.[32] However, others like Walter Kasper and Dermot Lane see the formula "on the third day" as a soteriological affirmation rather than a strictly historical one; it is not primarily a calendar or chronological date but an expression of the meaning of the resurrection of Jesus for our salvation. Lane notes that "on the third day" is a technical expression used in the Hebrew Scriptures to designate the day of deliverance and the dawning of salvation (Gen 22:4; Exod 19:1-11; Hos 6:1-3; Josh 3:2).[33] Good Friday, Easter, Ascension, and Pentecost form one single, indivisible mystery, particularly in John's Gospel, though Luke introduces a period of forty days between the resurrection and the ascension, at least in Acts.[34] Nichols grants that such a view of immediate resurrection might make sense if we say "that the time of the resurrection does not correspond with earthly time and that it is the form, not the matter, of the body that comes over into the resurrection."[35]

Some see the dogma of Mary's assumption of soul and body into glory as affirming as true in her case what is possible for all who die in Christ. Peter Phan, with reference to an article by Rahner, argues that the dogma "need not be seen as excluding the possibility of other human beings enjoying the same 'privilege.'"[36]

---

31. Robinette, *Grammars of Resurrection*, 169. N. T. Wright takes a similar position; see *Surprised by Hope: Rethinking Heaven, the Resurrection, and the Misison of the Church* (New York: HarperCollins, 2008), 249.

32. Nichols, *Death and Afterlife*, 148.

33. Lane, *Keeping Hope Alive*, 105; Pope Benedict argues for the third day as the day for the discovery of the empty tomb and the first encounter with the risen Jesus; it is the reason why the Christian community assembled for worship on the first day of the week; Pope Benedict XVI, *Jesus of Nazareth, Part II* (San Francisco: Ignatius, 2011), 258.

34. Kasper, *Jesus the Christ*, 146–48.

35. Nichols, *Death and Afterlife*, 148.

36. Phan, "Contemporary Context," 526; see also Karl Rahner, "The Interpretation of the Dogma of the Assumption," in *Theological Investigations*, vol. 1 (London: Darton, Longman and Todd, 1961), 225–26.

The Basis of Our Eschatological Hope

Having looked at different views on the intermediate state, we need to consider more carefully three contemporary ways of understanding the nature of our eschatological hope. Joseph Ratzinger's approach, much of which we have already reviewed, is primarily spiritual, rooted in the spiritual nature of the soul and in the promise in both the Old and New Testaments that our communion with God will be sustained beyond death. Brian Robinette, in his study of the "grammar" of the resurrection, focuses on the corporeality of grace and the social nature of the resurrection. Finally, perceiving a tension in Paul's letters, Dermot Lane suggests that Paul taught that for the individual living a life in Christ, the resurrection takes place at the moment of death, while he or she still looks forward to the coming together of all things in Christ at the end of time. We will consider each of these views.

Ratzinger: Immortality as Relationship

Ratzinger's basic insight is that we find in the Old Testament a growing awareness that communion with God is stronger than death. The view that it overcomes Sheol is evident in some of the later psalms, as we have already seen.

> Therefore my heart is glad, my soul rejoices;
> 　　my body also dwells secure,
> For your will not abandon me to Sheol,
> 　　nor let your faithful servant see the pit.
> You will show me the path to life,
> 　　abounding joy in your presence,
> 　　the delights at your right hand forever. (Ps 16:9-11)

He refers also to Psalm 73, which contrasts the afflictions of the just with the prosperity of the wicked, the arrogant who grow healthy and sleek, increasing their wealth while they scoff that God has no knowledge of their wickedness. But the just who trust in the Lord can be confident of God's care:

> With your counsel you guide me,
> 　　and at the end receive me with honor.
> Whom else have I in the heavens?
> 　　None beside you delights me on earth.
> Though my flesh and my heart fail,
> 　　God is the rock of my heart, my portion forever. (Ps 73:24-26)

Ratzinger also points to what he calls the "martyr literature," late books like Daniel 12:2 and 2 Maccabees that witness to belief in the resurrection of the dead, as well as the book of Wisdom, which borrows from Greek thought to envision the souls of the just preserved in God's hands, as we saw earlier (Wis 3:1-9). But what the Old Testament really stresses is an enduring relationship with God, even if it sometimes lacks the philosophical language to describe it; this confidence in a lasting communion with God for the just "operates neither with the concept of soul nor with the idea of resurrection." It is rooted in the experience of communion with God.[37]

In an appendix arguing for a continued life with the Lord between death and resurrection, Ratzinger maintains that the Christian concept of the soul is unique; it cannot be reduced to a borrowing from philosophical thought, though it has drawn upon earlier insights, purifying and transforming them, particularly in Aquinas's reformulation of Aristotle's formula of the soul as form of the body, adding the concept of spirit[38] with its capacity for relationship, as we saw earlier. This is Ratzinger's position: immortality is rooted in a relationship with God; it is not a natural capacity of the human. "Soul is nothing other than man's capacity for relatedness with truth, with love eternal," with the truth and love that we call "God."[39] We will look at the concept of the soul in the following chapter.

Robinette: The Corporeality of Grace

Brian Robinette speaks of the "corporeality of grace." He begins with a nod to Karl Rahner who once described Christians as "the most sublime of materialists" because they "neither can nor should conceive of any ultimate fullness of the spirit and of reality without thinking too of matter enduring as well in a state of final perfection."[40] Robinette's insight is fundamentality Pauline, based on Paul's use of *sōma pneumatikón*, a spiritual body. He understands Paul to mean not some radical self-transcendence that leaves bodily life behind but "a qualitatively new state of bodily life, one freed from corruption and alienation,"

---

37. Ratzinger, *Eschatology*, 87–91 at 90.

38. Ibid., 257; see appendix I, 241–60.

39. Ibid., 259.

40. Karl Rahner, "The Festival of the Future of the World," in *Theological Investigations*, vol. 7 (New York: Herder and Herder, 1971), 183.

emphasizing God's creative action "upon and within creation."[41] Thus resurrection means not dematerialization but rather material creation most fully realized.[42] From this perspective, as Ghislain Lafont points out, "the end-time will not be the removal of all duration, since duration is connatural to existence, but its transfiguration into total communication of God with humans and of humans with each other, in a world that has finally been reconciled."[43]

And indeed, from an eschatological perspective, or better, an apocalyptic eschatological perspective, that future is already breaking into the present, vivifying creation through the Spirit who raised Christ and dwells in our mortal bodies, moving us toward that day when we will experience the full redemption of our bodies (Rom 8:11, 22-23). Paul's contrast between *sōma psychikon* and *sōma pneumatikón* is not between two levels of human existence but between two modes of personal existence: living under one's own power or being wholly indwelt by God's *pneuma*.

Lane: Individual and General Resurrection

Lane begins by acknowledging the inadequacies of the dualistic anthropology of classical eschatology, especially the problem of what kind of life the soul separated from the body might enjoy. He argues that while the early Paul looked forward to the Parousia or second coming of Christ happening in his time (1 Thess 4:13-17), he later developed a theology of an interim period between the resurrection of Christ and his second coming. He saw the baptized as initiated mystically into Christ's paschal mystery, his death and resurrection (Rom 6:3-4, 11; Col 1:12): "For we who live are constantly being given up to death for the sake of Jesus, so that the life of Jesus may be manifested in our mortal flesh" (2 Cor 4:11).

Thus, baptism initiates a process of transformation in Christ that reaches an initial finality at the time of death. Lane appeals to Paul's image of the earthly tent giving way to "a dwelling not made with hands, eternal in heaven" (2 Cor 5:1), to the analogy of the seed that falls into the ground and dies, becoming the sheaf of wheat (1 Cor 15:37,

41. Robinette, *Grammars of Resurrection*, 153; see also 211.

42. Ibid., 158.

43. See Ghislain Lafont, *A Theological Journey: Christian Faith and Human Salvation* (Collegeville, MN: Liturgical Press, 2007), 81; also David Wilkinson, "Space-Time in Creation and New Creation," in *Christian Eschatology and the Physical Universe* (New York: T. & T. Clark International, 2010), 115–35.

42-44), to his talk of sharing in Christ's sufferings and being conformed to his death, that "I may attain the resurrection from the dead" (Phil 3:11), and to the promise of life through the Spirit given in baptism: "If the Spirit of the one who raised Jesus from the dead dwells in you, the one who raised Christ from the dead will give life to your mortal bodies also (Rom 8:11; see also Rom 8:14-17; 2 Cor 5:5). "What happens in death," Lane writes, "seems to go well beyond what might be called the immortality of the soul. There is more than continuity implied; there is also change (1 Cor 15:51-57; 2 Cor 3:18), newness (2 Cor 5:17), and transformation (1 Cor 15:42-43). "A real difference exists between the immortality of the soul which is about continuity and survival, and the resurrection of the body which is about the fulfilment and transformation of the individual."[44]

But there are many other texts in Paul that look forward to a future when creation itself shares in the glorious freedom of the children of God (Rom 8:23-23) and all things are summed up in Christ, both in heaven and on earth (Eph 1:10). When everything has been subjected to him, "then the Son himself will [also] be subjected to the one who subjected everything to him, so that God may be all in all" (1 Cor 15:28). To reconcile this tension within Paul, Lane suggests that the resurrection of the individual, already begun through baptism, takes place in death, while the second coming of Christ marks the fulfillment of all of Christ's work, gathering together all people, history, and creation itself: "The incompleteness of individual resurrection is overcome through what might be called a process of socialization and cosmic transformation that characterizes the end of time."[45] This raises the question of the social nature of the resurrection.

The Social Nature of the Resurrection

Against the individualistic tendency of so much of Western thought, caught up in the ideal of the autonomous self, an increasing number of theologians are emphasizing the social nature of the self and indeed of the resurrection. Dermot Lane critiques modern anthropology for its subject-centered self-consciousness, which has lost sight of God's

44. Dermot A. Lane, *Keeping Hope Alive*, 157.
45. Ibid., 158–59.

immanence to creation. He appeals to feminist critiques of the modern self that stress instead the radically relational, processive, and multipolar self, to the ecological movement that sees the earth itself as threatened by an excessive anthropocentrism, and to postmodern cosmologies that critique the removal of the self from creation.[46] Brian Robinette stresses that relation precedes identity both logically and temporally.[47]

Consider for a moment our radically social nature. Relationships are real; they can be creative, life-giving, or destructive. Each person comes from a relationship even prior to birth that joins two bodies in an intimate union, often loving but sometimes violent. From this develops the embryo, fetus, and ultimately the unborn child, formed by the union of egg and sperm, nourished by the blood of its mother, and later nursed at her breast. Each stage in the process is formative. Each of us is shaped by a multitude of relations even before we are born but also in home, family, community, and culture; and our lives become intertwined with the lives of others, for better or for worse. Some will open themselves to God's saving grace because of gracious acts of compassion, presence, or love mediated by others. Others may turn in on themselves, closing themselves off to grace, because interactions with others in home or environment have been hurtful, injurious, or violent. We do not come to heaven alone but accompanied by others, those we have helped or hindered on the journey to eternal life, whose lives are now intertwined inseparably with our own.

Ratzinger also stresses the social nature of the self, relating it to the biblical notion of the Body of Christ:

> Every human being exists in himself and outside himself: everyone exists simultaneously in other people. What happens in one individual has an effect upon the whole of humanity, and what happens in humanity happens in the individual. 'The Body of Christ' means that all human beings are one organism, the destiny of the whole the proper destiny of each. True enough, the decisive outcome of each person's life is settled in death, at the close of their earthly activity. . . . But his final place in the whole can be determined only when the total organism is complete, when the *passio* and *action* of history have come to their end.[48]

---

46. Ibid., 26–28.
47. Robinette, *Grammars of Resurrection*, 167.
48. Ratzinger, *Eschatology*, 190.

Robinette, following Ratzinger here, emphasizes the corporeal nature not just of our bodies but even of our identity. Our bodies are not some kind of appendage or add-on to our innermost self. He argues that I am my body, and my personal identity is rooted in my body, emerging out of my personal history, my loves and relationships (both positive and negative), the decisions I have made, and what I have suffered. Because of my embodied status, identity is consequent, not prior to my experience. My body is where salvation happens, and because my body is intertwined with other bodies in a constant interaction of the self and the other, my personal fulfillment or eschatological destiny is linked to their own. The resurrection of the body means the completion of my own narrative journey, including the effective history of my life upon others.[49]

This is perhaps Robinette's most difficult point to grasp, but it is also one of his most creative. His notion of the corporeality of grace means that the doctrine of the resurrection of the body is social and joins us inseparably to others. Relationality is the key, just as God's very being is to be in relation. Thus our eschatological fulfillment can only be understood and realized in relation to others and indeed to all of creation.[50] We do not enter eternity alone; we bring others with us, just as so many fellow travelers have played a significant role in our own journey. Robinette's way of expressing this is to say several times, echoing Karl Rahner, that eschatology is anthropology in the future tense.[51]

The Apocalyptic Imagination

To develop this social understanding of the resurrection, or in his words, its "practical-political character," Robinette calls for a retrieval of the apocalyptic imagination, which he finds developed in the work of Johann Baptist Metz and Edward Schillebeeckx.[52] He argues that too often theologians, including Rahner, have preferred to speak of eschatology instead of apocalyptic, as the latter suggests to people schooled in modernity troubling end-of-time speculations, sectarianism, and determinism. These characteristics often describe apocalyptic as a genre; it is otherworldly, highly symbolic, and complex. But focusing only on these

49. Robinette, *Grammars of Resurrection*, 164–68.

50. Ibid., 168.

51. Ibid., 159–77 at 165, 177; cf. Karl Rahner, "Theology and Anthropology," in *Theological Investigations*, vol. 9 (New York: Herder and Herder, 1972), 28–45.

52. Robinette, *Grammars of Resurrection*, 211.

characteristics risks missing the real power of the apocalyptic imagination, which brings the hope of God's transforming power and grace into the present social situation of victimization and oppression, effecting "a revolution in the imagination that could affirm the reality of an alternative, transcendent order in the face of large-scale chaos in the social-cultural world, usually as the result of domination from an external, imperial power."[53] In the words of H. H. Rowley, "the prophets foretold the future that should rise out of the present, while the apocalypticists foretold the future that should break into the present."[54]

Apocalyptic imagery can be found in the Synoptic Gospels, in the letters of Paul, and of course in the book of Revelation, the only example of a fully apocalyptic work in the New Testament. The death of Jesus on the cross is described in apocalyptic language by the Synoptics, particularly in Matthew's Gospel where apocalyptic motifs are particularly abundant but are modified in light of Matthew's Christology.[55] Matthew frequently describes Jesus as the Son of Man coming in judgment—some thirteen times, with Daniel 7 in the background. He describes darkness coming over the earth, the veil of the Temple's sanctuary being torn in two at the moment of his death, followed by earthquakes, the opening of tombs, and the bodies of saints rising up, entering the city, and appearing to many (Matt 27:51-53). The language of resurrection is itself apocalyptic language, as Michael Cook notes; it is "intended to signal God's vindication of the just in the face of persecution."[56] While theologians continue to argue about whether or not Jesus himself looked toward an apocalyptic fulfillment, his preaching of the reign of God, enacted through his exorcisms, miracles, table fellowship, and proclaiming the forgiveness of sins, meant that God's saving power was already breaking into the lives of others.

Paul's most obvious apocalyptic passage is his description of the Rapture, when the trumpet will sound and the dead will rise: "The dead in Christ will rise first. Then we who are alive, who are left, will be caught up together with them in the clouds to meet the Lord in the air" (1 Thess

53. Ibid., 197; see also David J. Leigh, *Apocalyptic Patterns in Twentieth-Century Fiction* (Notre Dame: University of Notre Dame Press, 2008).

54. Harold H. Rowley, *The Relevance of Apocalyptic* (New York: Association Press, 1964), 38.

55. Paul O'Callaghan, *The Christological Assimilation of the Apocalypse* (Dublin: Four Courts Press, 2004), 232.

56. Michael Cook, *Trinitarian Christology* (New York: Paulist, 2010), 36.

4:16-17), a passage so dear to conservative evangelicals. His early letters give evidence that he believed that the world was passing away, as he advises the members of the church at Corinth not to marry in order to better prepare for the coming of the Lord (1 Cor 7:29-31). But Paul also writes in less end-time terms. He sees the resurrection of Jesus as evidence that God's salvation has appeared, revealing God's mysterious wisdom, hidden through the ages and now revealed through the Spirit (1 Cor 2:6-13). Most of all, he teaches that our salvation is to find its full realization not in this life but in the resurrection (Rom 6:3-5) and in the Parousia (1 Cor 15:23-28).

Perhaps what is most important to remember about apocalyptic is that the Greek word *apocalypsis* means not the end of the world but revelation, usually a revelation of God's justice for those suffering persecution. According to John J. Collins, a movement can be called apocalyptic "if it shared the conceptual framework of the genre, endorsing a worldview in which supernatural revelation, the heavenly world, and eschatological judgment played essential parts."[57] A poetic literary form that uses images and symbols, apocalyptic is always rooted in concrete social and historical circumstances, providing a vision that moves others to action: "It is far more congenial to the pragmatic tendency of liberation theology, which is not engaged in the pursuit of truth but in the dynamics of motivation and the exercise of political power."[58]

An article about South African Anglican Archbishop Desmond Tutu offers a wonderful example of the power of the apocalyptic imagination. Shortly after the murder of black African leader Steve Biko in 1977, Tutu declared that white rule in South Africa was finished: "The powers of injustice, of oppression, of exploitation, have done their worst, and they have lost. . . . They have lost because they are immoral and wrong, and our God . . . is a God of justice and liberation and goodness. Our cause . . . must triumph because it is moral and just and right."[59] Tutu was saying that the apartheid system was doomed; it was evil and would fall because God's justice was inexorable, already revealed in the resurrection of Jesus.

---

57. John J. Collins, *The Apocalyptic Imagination: An Introduction to Jewish Apocalyptic Literature*, 2nd ed. (Grand Rapids, MI: William B. Eerdmans, 1998), 13; see "The Apocalyptic Genre," 1–42; see also David S. Russell, *Divine Disclosure: An Introduction to Jewish Apocalyptic* (Minneapolis: Fortress, 1992).

58. Collins, *The Apocalyptic Imagination*, 283.

59. Alex Perry, "The Laughing Bishop," *Time* 176 (October 11, 2010): 42.

Thus, the apocalyptic imagination is more powerful than an eschatological imagination alone. Eschatology looks toward the future, promising fulfillment of history; apocalyptic brings the future into the present with a hope that energizes. It sustains fidelity and makes resistance to tyranny possible. This is what Johann Baptist Metz calls the "dangerous memory" of the passion, death, and resurrection of Jesus:

> This *memoria Jesu Christi* is not a memory which deceptively dispenses Christians from the risks involved in the future. It is not a middle-class counter-figure to hope. On the contrary, it anticipates the future as a future of those who are oppressed, without hope and doomed to fail. It is therefore a dangerous and at the same time liberating memory that oppresses and questions the present because it reminds us not of some open future, but precisely this future and because it compels Christians constantly to change themselves so that they are able to take this future into account.[60]

Metz contrasts this apocalyptic consciousness (which he calls eschatological time) with evolutionary time, or again, he contrasts faith time with rational time. The former allows for imminent expectation of God's grace breaking in; it empowers the imagination, while the latter—evolutionary or rational time—is a closed system, a view of time as evolving toward infinity without grace.[61]

James Alison has a different take, but his conclusions are similar. He sees apocalyptic imagery as characterized by certain dualities—heaven and earth, this world and the world to come, the good and the bad, the righteous and the impious, the afflicted and their persecutors—all of which will be reversed in the world to come, but this nonetheless represents an imagination still stuck in the notion of a violent God who brings about an ultimate eschatological vengeance for victims. He sees Jesus as subverting this apocalyptic imagination with a more prophetic eschatological imagination, subverting the apocalyptic dualities, redefining them in terms of the forgiving victim, the crucified and risen one who becomes present in history and offers a new life not bounded by death. Thus our

---

60. Johann Baptist Metz, *Faith in History and Society: Toward a Practical Fundamental Theology*, trans. David Smith (New York: Seabury, 1980), 90; see also Bruce T. Morrill, *Anamnesis as Dangerous Memory: Political and Liturgical Theology in Dialogue* (Collegeville, MN: Liturgical Press, 2000).

61. Ibid., 170–76; see also Robinette, *Grammars of Resurrection*, 213–15.

very understanding of time is changed; it is no longer seen as moving toward a violent end, but the end comes to be a principle in time, empowering his disciples by bringing future hope into the present, not unlike Metz's concept of the dangerous *memoria Jesu Christi*.[62]

Conclusion

From the beginning, the early Christians proclaimed the resurrection of Jesus, first in kerygmatic formulae and later in more elaborate narratives or stories centered on the discovery of the empty tomb and the appearances to the disciples, designed to help others come to Easter faith. The theological character of the Easter stories suggests that there is something nonobjectifiable about the risen Jesus; he comes and goes at will, passes through walls and doors, and is not recognized.

Rather than an objective event open to the neutral observer, his resurrection is more properly an eschatological event, one that takes place on the other side of time and history, though it has left its mark in his self-disclosure to the disciples and in their testimony. For Paul, the resurrection of Jesus means that the *eschaton* or last age has already begun. He calls Jesus the "last Adam," the "firstfruits" of the resurrection of the dead. Jesus' resurrection shows God's solidarity with all the victims of history. An apocalyptic eschatology sees God's power breaking into history, heralding a new age, changing our concept of time, and promising the vindication all the victims of injustice. But if the *eschaton* has in some way already occurred, "its final actualization among human beings is yet to take place."[63]

In the *eschaton* Christ will reign, putting his enemies under his feet until the last enemy, death itself, is destroyed, and with all things subjected to Christ, the Son himself will be subjected to God so that God may be all in all. Thus Paul's argument envisions a return of humanity and creation itself to God through Christ (1 Cor 15:20-28), a setting free or transformation of creation along with the children of God (cf. Rom 8:22-23).

If the Middle Ages saw considerable speculation about how the risen body was constituted, another tradition with roots in classic Hellenistic

---

62. See Alison, *Raising Abel*, 124–27.

63. Don E. Saliers, *Worship as Theology: Foretaste of Glory Divine* (Nashville: Abingdon, 1994), 51.

thought focused on the soul. Separated from the body by death, the soul was the principle of continuity between earthly life and the resurrection of the body, even if a soul without a body was considered less than a whole person and Aquinas found it difficult to explain how it could know or understand.

Finally, we saw that not a few contemporary thinkers, reacting against the solipsistic individualism of modern thought, see the resurrection as having a social dimension. Salvation is about far more than confessing Jesus and getting "saved." Even if the resurrection will touch each of us individually, our own self and destiny, far from being autonomous, are shaped, conditioned by, and dependent on—for better or for worse—all our embodied relationships. Our relations with family and friends, our past experience, our sexuality, our relations with the poor—all these make up the trajectory of our lives.

In asking the anthropological question about the basis of our eschatological hope, we considered three different views. Ratzinger rejects the idea of a resurrection in death, holding with considerable force instead for an intermediate state between death and the resurrection of the body. Focusing on the promise of both the Old and New Testaments that our communion with God survives beyond death, he roots our capacity for a relationship with God in our spiritual nature, in our soul or nature as embodied spirit. Robinette, following Paul, stresses that bodily life will not be left behind in the resurrection and indeed that the future is already breaking into the world and our own bodies through the Spirit. Lane's approach is similar: he too sees the power of Christ's resurrection already transforming the baptized, reaching an initial fulfillment in our own resurrection at the moment of death, while all creation waits its ultimate fulfillment at Christ's second coming. On this day God's justice will be revealed for all those who have suffered in history, and every tear will be wiped away (cf. Rev 21:4).

5

The *Eschata* and the *Eschaton*

In the first chapter of this work we spoke of the loss of the eschato-logical imagination that occurred in the latter half of the first millennium. From the seventh century on, the expectation for the coming of God's salvation in its fullness faded as Christian preaching, art, and theology increasingly centered on fear of judgment and the fires that would purify the dead, what would be known as purgatory. Thus what emerged was an increasingly individualistic understanding of eschatology, a fearful moment or day of judgment, followed by either eternal bliss or damnation. The focus was on the individual. The *eschaton* gave way to the *eschata*, the last things.

The rise of modernity and the emergence of the solitary self only heightened this soteriological individualism, so that for many today salvation is reduced to "saving" one's soul, gaining access to heaven, or alternatively, being confined for eternity to the fires of hell. Since eschatology includes the personal dimensions of our destiny, we will begin this chapter by considering the concept of the soul. Then we will move to the *eschata*, the traditional last things—death and judgment, heaven and hell—and finally to the *eschaton*, the fullness of our salvation.

The Soul

In the Western philosophical tradition, "soul" refers to the life principle of a sentient being, expressed by the Hebrew *nepesh* (life or breath) or the Greek *psychē* (life, spirit, consciousness). But soul also has the sense of "spirit," something that goes beyond the simply material. It is the soul that is revealed in that capacity and penchant of our minds to always move beyond the concrete things we know, to ask questions: Where does being come from, when did it begin, will it end, and why is there anything at all?

Focusing on its spiritual nature, Ratzinger says that the soul is nothing other than our capacity for relatedness with truth, with love eternal.[1] Terence Nichols speaks of the soul as the subject of personal consciousness or personal identity, a subject capable of personal, subjective experience from its relation to the body, to others, and to God. It can survive the death of the body not because of its essential nature but because God has entered into a personal relationship with it, for as St. Paul says, "the gifts and calling of God are irrevocable" (Rom 11:29).[2]

This spiritual dimension of our being is best disclosed for us in the experience of transcendence. We are aware of a transcendental knowledge, an a posteriori knowledge that is awakened by our experience of things in the world but reaches beyond it. We can think of examples in which transcendence is disclosed in our self-consciousness, in reflective intelligence. I know that organisms die, that matter breaks down, that energy diminishes, moving the universe toward entropy. Thus, I reach in my self-awareness beyond the continuum of my experience to the death that will apparently be its end to ask if there is a life beyond death and the decay that accompanies it. In doing so, I am raising a question not directly experienced: Is there a light beyond the darkness before and after my life? Is there something beyond the finitude I both experience and question?

Even grasping the finite as finite suggests an awareness of transcendence, for if the mind did not transcend the limits of the finite, the finite could not be known as such. The two, the finite and the infinite, are not mutually exclusive but imply each other. "The finite cannot be known without the Infinite or, to put it differently, the finite is nothing without the Infinite."[3] What this experience of transcendence suggests, with our

---

1. Joseph Ratzinger, *Eschatology: Death and Eternal Life*, 2nd ed., trans. by Michael Waldstein (Washington, DC: Catholic University of America Press, 1988), 259.

2. Terence Nichols, *Death and Afterlife: A Theological Introduction* (Grand Rapids, MI: Brazos, 2010), 129–31 at 131.

3. Frederiek Depoortere, *The Death of God: An Investigation into the History of the Western Concept of God* (London and New York: T. & T. Clark, 2008), 167; see also Anselm K. Min, "Hegel's Absolute: Transcendent or Immanent?" *The Journal of Religion* 56/1 (1976): 68–71.

minds reaching out, our questions moving constantly beyond our limited knowledge, is that we are in some way oriented toward Being itself, not the things of the world that we know but Being as such, the mystery that is beyond and in some way grasped, "pre-apprehended," in all our conscious activity.[4] Our knowing takes place against a horizon of Being that is never exhausted by the beings we know.

The experience of transcendence points to what philosophy has understood by the concept of the soul. Ratzinger's treatment of Greek thought on the subject is helpful for showing how diverse it actually was. For the popular characterization of the so-called Platonic view of the soul as imprisoned in the body, Ratzinger points to the Orphic mystery tradition, a tradition far from Greek in its origin. Plato transformed this tradition, placing immortality in a religious, mytho-poetic context that provided the point of departure for his principal concern, a philosophy of justice. But according to Ratzinger, he failed to develop a unified account of the nature of the soul, including its relation to the body, leaving his successors "wandering in the philosophical landscape pitted with problems."[5] Thus he dismisses the traditional notion of a Hellenic-Platonic dualism as "something of a theologian's fantasy."[6]

If Plato treated the soul in a religious context, Aristotle understood it in purely philosophical terms; he saw the soul as an organic principle, a form bound to its matter and unable to endure apart from it. What was truly spiritual in the human person was *nous*, not something personal and individual but rather ours through participation in a transcendent, divine principle. One thinks immediately of the medieval Averroists who held that all humans shared the same intellect.

For the Stoics, the soul consisted of fire, the lightest of all the elements, and at death it returned to its source in the great fire. Thus the Stoic view was basically materialistic. Individuality did not survive death. Similarly, Plotinus privileged unity over diversity; he divided the world into three substances: the One, *nous*, and soul. His spiritual doctrine, really a kind of spirituality, challenged human beings to resist the soul's descent into the illusion of plurality by ascending to its true nature as unity. But in this ascent, the illusion of individuality disappears.

---

4. Karl Rahner, *Foundations of Christian Faith: An Introduction to the Idea of Christianity* (New York: Seabury, 1978), 33

5. Ratzinger, *Eschatology*, 143.

6. Ibid., 145.

Ratzinger's conclusion is that the church did not inherit a clear concept of the afterlife from the Greek world. The Christian view developed from the Jewish view of the life of the dead in Sheol, given new meaning by the New Testament's focus on the person of Jesus and his resurrection. Yet the early church lacked a unified terminology. Most common was the language of the soul or spirit, which emerged late in the Jewish tradition, as we have seen. Ratzinger adds the caution that for the Gnostics, whose thought was such a danger to early Christianity, soul (*psychē*) was placed on the lowest level of human existence, in comparison to the "pneumatics," the enlightened people of the spirit.[7]

It was Aquinas who fused the Aristotelian notion of soul as form, inseparable from body, with the idea of spirit, with its capacity for a relationship with God. [8] Ratzinger draws here on the work of Anton Pegis, who in a commentary on the *Summa Contra Gentiles* II, chapter 56, argues that Aquinas was clearly moving beyond Aristotle's thought in holding that an intellectual substance, the soul, could be joined to a body as its substantial form. In Pegis's words, "Revelation had corrected philosophical errors and it had given answers that were beyond the scope and the expectation of philosophy."[9] As spirit, the soul could exist apart from the body, but as the form of the body it remained incomplete. Its ability to know after that separation became problematic, as did its ability to maintain its sense of personal identity, dependent on the body's memory, as we saw earlier in reference to Aquinas.

Aquinas's notion of a spiritual soul was a great achievement, even if it left at least partially unresolved the question of personal identity in the soul separated from the body by death, as we saw earlier.

The *Eschata*

In talking about the experience of transcendence, rooted in the spiritual dimension of our nature, we considered the questions we ask about what lies beyond the end of our lives. Is there life beyond death? In the same way, having experienced the love of another, the joy of being

---

7. Ibid., 147.

8. Ibid., 149.

9. Anton Pegis, "Some Reflections on *Summa Contra Gentiles* II, 56," in *An Etienne Gilson Tribute*, ed. Charles J. O'Neill (Milwaukee: Marquette University Press, 1959), 184.

known, held, and cherished, we ask about the possibility of a love that lies beyond the loves that are always imperfect and must one day end. Is there an Other, a Thou, one who holds me in an embrace, who knows my deepest longings and fears, who offers a love that is unending? And will we be worthy of that love, able to respond in some way to the One who has first loved us? What about death and judgment?

Death

It is inevitable that each of us must one day die, no matter how much our culture tries to deny the reality of death. Our modern culture would just as soon ignore it. Ernest Becker's *The Denial of Death* is a classic. Arguing that the fear of death is universal, Becker's book is an effort, ultimately unsuccessful, to bring together in a post-Freudian world psychology and what he calls a "mythico-religious perspective."[10] From a less psychoanalytic perspective, our culture tries to "manage" death, and the physical decline that so often precedes it, to make it as unobtrusive as possible. Our elderly are often hidden away, cared for in retirement communities or "managed care" facilities. An increasing number of European countries and states in the US have "right to die" laws that allow for euthanasia, legal protections for individuals to authorize their physicians to administer life-ending drugs. And while we seek to disguise the reality of death, there is a corresponding lack of respect for the sacred character of life, with over a million abortions per year in the US, an easy tolerance of the death penalty, now outlawed by most nations of the world, and an unwillingness on the part of so many to support health care for the poor.

Perhaps the denial of death and the inability to recognize the sacredness of life are related. For death is not unrelated to life; it brings our life journey to its culmination, or better, to a point of transition. As the preface to the Catholic Mass of Christian Burial prays,

> Indeed for your faithful, Lord,
> life is changed not ended,
> and, when this earthly dwelling turns to dust,
> an eternal dwelling is made ready for them in heaven.

So death is part of life. It is to be accepted even in its diminishments. The theology of the fundamental option suggests that every decision made

---

10. Ernest Becker, *The Denial of Death* (New York: Free Press, 1973), xi.

over a lifetime shapes the person we become, opening us to others and to God or making us the center of our life, thus determining our fundamental orientation. Rather than a juridical focus on sinful acts, its approach is more psychological, recognizing the complex nature of moral consciousness, the social construction of the self, and our capacity for relationships or ability to live without them. As Karl Rahner says, death is the event in which a person becomes his or her definitive self.[11]

In dying, a person acts out of that fundamental option one more time, reaching out in trust and love to that mysterious Other who is God or drawing into the self where the person has been most comfortable and at home. Ladislaus Boros describes it as the person's first completely personal act, *"the place above all others for the awakening of consciousness, for freedom, for the encounter with God, for the final decision about eternal destiny."*[12]

Still, dying is never easy. Those who have accompanied friends or family members in their last days know how they are tested. Some are fearful, others are defiant or in denial. Persons whose lives have been characterized by a deep faith often find it difficult to pray. Others manifest a deep peace, opening themselves to the God who has always been at the center of their lives. Some go through many of these moments or stages. But certainly the God who has called us into being and continues to sustain us, even if not sensed in these final moments, is close. Indeed, God may be closest when apparently most absent, as in the experience of Jesus, God's only-begotten Son, the beloved who called out from the agony of the cross, "My God, my God, why have you forsaken me" (Mark 15:34), the Jesus who said in dying, "Father, into your hands I commend my spirit" (Luke 23:46).

Last Judgment

The idea of a last judgment of all peoples and nations developed under the influence of late Jewish apocalyptic. It often has cosmic dimensions. As we saw in chapter 2, Daniel 12:1-3 sees those raised up "at the end of days" (Dan 12:13) separated according to moral categories, some to shine brightly like the stars, others to be an everlasting horror and dis-

---

11. Karl Rahner, "Death," in *Encyclopedia of Theology: The Concise* Sacramentum Mundi (New York: Seabury, 1975), 329; see also Rahner, *On the Theology of Death* (New York: Herder and Herder, 1961).

12. Ladislaus Boros, *The Mystery of Death* (New York: Herder and Herder, 1965), 84; italics in original.

grace. In late Jewish apocalyptic the "shades" of the dead in the earlier tradition became "souls" or "spirits" who maintain a relationship with God after death. In 2 Esdras 7, Sheol has become an intermediary state where the dead await the resurrection and final judgment and the righteous are separated from the sinners, some of whom must still receive punishment for their sins (1 Enoch 22).[13] But what is most characteristic of Jewish apocalyptic literature is the doctrine of the Last Judgment: "It is *the* great event towards which the whole universe is moving and which will vindicate once and for all God's righteous purpose for men and all creation."[14]

In the New Testament, there are references to "the day of the Son of Man" (Luke 17:30), a vision reflective of the Old Testament Day of Yahweh, or to the "day of judgment" (Matt 10:15; 12:36). There are frequent references to the Son of Man coming in glory or being revealed, modeled on Daniel 7:13 and possibly used by Jesus himself (Matt 26:64; Mark 14:62; Luke 9:26; 21:27; 2 Cor 1:14; Phil 2:16). A most dramatic passage is Matthew 25:31-46, where the Son of Man comes to judge the nations, separating the sheep from the goats on the basis of their care for the poor. Elsewhere he is described as coming on the clouds to gather the elect (Matt 24:30-31; Mark 13:26-27).

Not identical but related is the idea of the Parousia (the word means "presence" or "arrival"), the coming of the risen Christ as savior and judge. The Parousia will be preceded by signs in the heavens (Mark 13:24; Matt 24:29; Luke 21:25-27). In one of Paul's early letters it is announced by an archangel and the blast of a trumpet (1 Thess 4:16), after which the living will be lifted up ("raptured," for some evangelicals) to meet the Lord in the air (1 Thess 4:17). Later letters focus more on the resurrection of the dead, when Christ hands over the kingdom to God (1 Cor 15:21-24), while the community prays for his coming with the invocation *Maranatha* (1 Cor 16:22). The day of the Lord will come like a thief, and the heavens will pass away with a roar (2 Pet 3:10). Not even the Son of Man knows the exact day or hour (Mark 13:32).

The Johannine writings do not speak of the Parousia, and the idea of judgment is presented differently, with typical Johannine paradox. Jesus was not sent to judge but to save the world (John 3:17; 12:47), but those who refuse to believe have already been judged (3:18; 5:24), while those

13. See D. S. Russell, *The Method and Message of Jewish Apocalyptic* (Philadelphia: Westminster, 1964), 357–65.

14. Ibid., 380.

who have done wicked deeds will come to the resurrection of condemnation (John 5:29). There remains an ambiguity as to who will function as judge, God (Matt 6:14; Rom 2:3) or Jesus (Matt 25:31-46; 2 Cor 5:10), but the idea that the wicked must one day face judgment is everywhere.

Terence Nichols raises the question of justification, specifically justification by faith, in the context of judgment. For Martin Luther, the doctrine of justification by faith is the gospel answer to souls fearful of God's judgment and unsure of their own righteousness. Catholics and Reformers argued about the relation between faith and works, whether justification is imputed or transformative through the infusion of faith, hope, and love, the role of merit, and, we might add, whether or not our freedom is involved in accepting the grace of justification. While Luther's position is ambiguous, Calvin's is perfectly clear. The will is corrupt, the result of original sin, unable to choose the good; justification is God's work, leading Calvin to the unhappy doctrine of double predestination.

Nichols shows how Matthew's Gospel teaches us in the Sermon on the Mount (Matt 5–7) that we must have a higher righteousness, expressed in love, that we will be judged on the basis of our care for the hungry, the thirsty, the poor, the sick, and the imprisoned (Matt 25:31-46). In Luke's Gospel, conversion, a *metanoia* that puts God and God's kingdom first and is manifested not just in words but in deeds, is the key to justification and salvation. And Paul, who never uses the expression "faith alone," insists that we are not saved by works of the law, that faith in Christ "is not merely verbal profession of belief; it includes the active living out of faith, or what he calls 'the obedience of faith' (Rom 16:26)."[15] But we cannot do this alone; we need a mediator, someone who brings God's grace, the Holy Spirit whom he refers to as both the Spirit of God and as the Spirit of Christ (Rom 8).[16]

If both Catholics and most Protestants are agreed today that we cannot be saved without faith in God and Christ, or better, without God's grace in Christ, there is not yet full agreement, particularly with evangelicals. As Scot McKnight writes, "an increasing tension remains among evangelicals about who gets to set the terms: Jesus or Paul. In other words, will we center our gospel teaching and living on 'the kingdom' or 'justification by faith'?"[17]

---

15. Nichols, *Death and Afterlife*, 151–58 at 156.
16. Ibid., 157.
17. Scot McKnight, "Jesus vs. Paul," *Christianity Today* 54/12 (2010): 26.

Unpopular as the idea of having to one day stand before the bar of God's judgment may be, it is an idea deeply rooted in both the Jewish and Christian Scriptures. Edward Schillebeeckx admits to having reservations about believing everybody will be saved; in spite of our silence about hell, eternal damnation, and judgment, it trivializes "the drama of the real course of events in the conflict between oppressed and oppressors, between the good and the evil in our human history."[18] The idea of judgment says that evil does not have the last word.

Still, we can understand the language of a last judgment, whether "particular" at the hour of our death or "general" at the end of time, as analogical. Drawing on the biblical tradition, we are arguing about what remains in many ways a mystery. For Ratzinger, Christ who is sheer salvation inflicts perdition on no one. What happens in death is that a human being "emerges into the light of full reality and truth. He takes up that place which is truly his by right."[19] We become the person we have determined ourselves to be, accepting or rejecting God's grace, as we shall see in the next section.

Hell

We need to say at the beginning that heaven and hell are asymmetrical concepts. That is to say, they are not on the same level.[20] Karl Rahner says that statements about heaven and those about hell are not parallel statements: "Since we are living in the eschaton of Jesus Christ . . . we know in our Christian faith . . . the history of salvation as a whole will reach a positive conclusion for the human race through God's own powerful grace."[21] While hell remains a possibility for those who definitively reject God's love, the church has never taught that anyone is actually in hell. Even more, the mystery of the incarnation, of God's love revealed in the story of Jesus, suggests a profound solidarity on the part of God not just with humankind but with creation. If the Christians in the Middle Ages lived in fear of the Last Judgment, today we have a better sense that while freedom means that we can always decide to live in isolation from God and others, we live in a world where grace abounds.

---

18. Edward Schillebeeckx, *Church: The Human Story of God* (New York: Crossroad, 1990), 136.

19. Ratzinger, *Eschatology*, 205–6.

20. Schillebeeckx, *Church*, 138; Dermot A. Lane, *Keeping Hope Alive: Stirrings in Christian Theology* (New York: Paulist, 1996), 137–38.

21. Rahner, *Foundations of Christian Faith*, 435.

The popular image of hell comes from the Aramaic word *Gehenna*, a shortened form of the "valley of the son of Hinnom." Located on the outskirts of Jerusalem, the modern Wadi er Rababi at the southern extremity of the hill of Zion, the place originally was a cultic shrine where human sacrifice was offered (2 Kgs 23:10; 2 Chr 28:3). Jeremiah cursed it (Jer 7:31-33), and Trito-Isaiah, without naming it, described it as the place where those who rebelled against Yahweh would end up, supplying images of fire and torment: "Their worm shall not die, nor their fire be extinguished; and they shall be abhorrent to all mankind" (Isa 66:24). Though the idea of a place of punishment for the wicked first appears in the noncanonical Jewish apocalyptic literature, specifically in 1 Enoch 22,[22] as we saw earlier, this image of the worm and the fire appears in other extrabiblical books: Assumption of Moses 10:19; Apocalypse of Baruch 59:10; Esdras 7:36. Thus the idea of a place of punishment after death came together with Gehenna, and it appears frequently in the rabbinical literature as a pit of fire, though the rabbis often saw the possibility of annihilation or eventual release. The English word "hell" comes from the German *Hel*, "place of the dead."

Dermot Lane, citing two parables and a saying of Jesus in which we can be confident that we hear his voice, says that the principal case for hell is to be found in the parable of the sheep and goats (Matt 25:31-46), the parable of the talents (Matt 25:14-30), and the reference to the unforgivable sin against the Holy Spirit that carries eternal guilt (Mark 3:29; Matt 12:32).[23]

Beyond that, the image of Gehenna appears frequently in the New Testament. It is a place of fire (Matt 5:22; 18:90) that is unquenchable (Mark 9:43), a pit into which the wicked are cast (Matt 5:29; Mark 9:45), where "their worm does not die, and the fire is not quenched" (Mark 9:48). The image of fire is used frequently; sinners will be punished in an eternal fire (Matt 18:8) prepared for the devil and his angels (Matt 25:41). Gehenna does not appear in John; the judgment that comes on sinners (John 3:8; 5:24; 12:31) excludes them from eternal life (John 5:29; 8:24; 10:28). For Paul, the impious are condemned to eternal destruction (2 Thess 1:9), sinners have no share in the kingdom of God (1 Cor 6:10; Gal 5:19-21), and the enemies of the cross are doomed to destruction (Phil 3:19). The book of Revelation also uses the image of a "pool of fire"

---

22. Russell, *The Method and Message of Jewish Apocalyptic*, 365.

23. Lane, *Keeping Hope Alive*, 141.

for those who exclude themselves from the book of life, thus meeting with a "second death" (Rev 20:14-15).

How should we understand these mytho-poetic images of fire and torment that have fascinated Christian artists over the centuries? Think, for example, of the work of Hieronymus Bosch. Does God condemn the unjust to eternal torment? Is there a hell? Does God punish? Conservative Protestant websites continue to blast Pope John Paul II, supposedly for having denied the existence of hell in one of his Wednesday audiences, after he pointed out that heaven, hell, and purgatory are states of being rather than places. Certainly God does not inflict suffering and anguish on people, either in this world or in the next. The suffering and alienation our sins bring into our lives is punishment enough. As creator and sustainer, God wants only our good, calling all men and women to communion in the life of the Father, Son, and Spirit. At the same time, it is a basic principle of the spiritual life that God always respects our freedom; God can elicit our love but cannot force us to respond with love to the one who has first loved us any more than we can force another to love us. Love is always a gift, freely given and freely received. According to Ratzinger, "Christ inflicts pure perdition on no one. In himself, he is pure salvation. Anyone who is with him has entered the space of deliverance and salvation."[24]

But we are free to refuse God's love, to focus only on ourselves, closing ourselves to the author of life and source of all goodness by placing ourselves first. This is the root nature of sin, the refusal to acknowledge the Creator (cf. Gen 3:5). To die in that state is hell, the eternal alienation from the one whose presence our hearts have ignored, to live in the isolation of our own self-centeredness. It means "the darkness that results from freely chosen negative introversion and self-isolation."[25] In one of his audiences, Pope John Paul II described this rejection of God's love and forgiveness as what Christian doctrine means when it speaks of eternal hell or damnation. It is not a punishment imposed from outside by God but the development of the premises that people have already set in life. Hell is not a place but the state of those who freely and definitively separate themselves from God.[26]

---

24. Ratzinger, *Eschatology*, 205.

25. Lane, *Keeping Hope Alive*, 140.

26. John Paul II, general audience, Wednesday 28 July 1999, nos. 1 and 3; http:// www.vatican.va/holy_father/john_paul_ii/audiences/1999/documents /hf_jp-ii_aud_28071999_en.html.

From Origen on, there have been church fathers who have expressed the hope that all eventually will be saved—the general *apokatastasis* or recapitulation. This has long been a tradition in Eastern Christianity, and Saint Thérèse of Lisieux was supposed to have said, "I believe in hell but I think that it is empty." Hans Urs von Balthasar has asked if somehow all might be saved.[27] Edward Schillebeeckx has expressed reservations about this notion of universal salvation, as we saw earlier.

Schillebeeckx argues that it makes little sense to imagine the just living, so to speak, "next door" to those who do not share in the kingdom of God. Pope Benedict XVI says something similar in his encyclical *Spe Salvi*; citing Dostoyevsky, he says that in the end, evildoers "do not sit at table at the eternal banquet beside their victims without distinction, as though nothing had happened" (no. 44). Communion with God and solidarity with others represent a bond that cannot be destroyed by death (what we used to call the "state of grace"). Scripture speaks of this as eternal life. But those whose lives have radically contradicted solidarity with other human beings, and thus with God, cannot share in eternal life. They have no room for others, no capacity for relationality. That is the meaning of hell—not eternal torture, but also not sharing in God's gift of everlasting life. In other words, those who have no relation with God do not survive their own deaths or share in the resurrection.[28] This position is often called "annihilationism." Others, however, argue that it goes against the idea of the God of Jesus. As Lane says, "there is something incongruous about affirming God as a God of the living alongside a hypothesis about hell as the annihilation of people."[29]

Purgatory

The concept of purgatory expresses the belief that those who die will go through purification either for "venial" sins or for the temporal punishment due to sins already forgiven. While not explicitly in Scripture, the concept is grounded in "the holy and pious" practice of praying for the dead in the late Old Testament (2 Macc 12:45) and practiced by the early Christians, particularly in their celebration of the Eucharist, with evidence going back to the second century. Tertullian (d. 220) in the West

---

27. Hans Urs von Balthasar, *Dare We Hope That All Men Be Saved?* (San Francisco: Ignatius, 1988); see also John R. Sachs, "Current Eschatology: Universal Salvation and the Problem of Hell," *Theological Studies* 52 (1991): 227–54.

28. Schillebeeckx, *Church*, 137–38.

29. Lane, *Keeping Hope Alive*, 143.

in his story of St. Perpetua praying for her dead brother Dinocrates and Clement of Alexandria (d. ca. 211) in the East who spoke of a purifying and educative fire contributed to the development of the concept, though Clement's view represented a synthesis of Christianity and Hellenism.[30] Augustine was convinced of the importance of praying for the dead, partly because of the long tradition of the Latin church, but also because he believed that the dead still belonged to time, not eternity, and therefore were not separated from the church. Some of the dead would experience the "temporal" punishment for their sins, while others had already experienced it in this life. But he believed that those condemned to punishment immediately after death could win forgiveness by the prayers of the church or by its offering of the Eucharist.[31]

By the eighth century, various ideas about prayer, intercession, and purgation for the dead came together as a place or prolonged stage in the afterlife.[32] Purgatory did not receive formal doctrinal expression until the thirteenth century. Both the Second Council of Lyons (1274) and the Council of Florence (1439) affirmed the doctrine in the context of disagreements with the East. While the Greeks accepted the Western practice of interceding for the dead with prayers, good works, and Masses offered on their behalf, they denied that punishment took place after death. In the sixteenth century, purgatory was a point of difference between Catholics and the Reformers; arguing the sufficiency of Christ's sacrifice, the Reformers rejected the practice of intercession on their behalf. And there were certainly abuses in Luther's time—witness the controversy over indulgences. The Council of Trent simply reaffirmed praying for the dead, "following the sacred writings and the ancient tradition of the Fathers," that there is a purgatory, and that the souls "are aided by the suffrages of the faithful and chiefly by the acceptable sacrifice of the altar" (DS 1820). While the Catholic tradition has long stressed expiation for sins, today the emphasis is more on purification of all that keeps us from union with God, thus of our love, which often remains imperfect and self-centered.

The practice of praying for the dead implies a communion in the Body of Christ that is not limited to our earthly existence. Similarly, because

---

30. Ratzinger, *Eschatology*, 226; see also Isabel Moreira, *Heaven's Purge: Purgatory in Late Antiquity* (New York: Oxford University Press, 2010), 25–27.

31. Brian E. Daley, *The Hope of the Early Church* (Cambridge: Cambridge University Press, 1991), 138–39; Moreira traces Augustine's "cautious views on the efficacy of prayer for relieving postmortem suffering" in *Heaven's Purge*, 36.

32. Moreira, *Heaven's Purge*, 6.

of this nontemporal communion, we pray for suicides and those who died suddenly in tragic accidents; they are never beyond hope. To this day, most Protestants do not pray for the dead; instead, they celebrate their lives or entrance into bliss. But the Lutheran-Catholic common statement "The Hope of Eternal Life" sees a growing unity in regard to practices for those who have died in Christ. It notes that Catholic and many Lutheran funeral liturgies, celebrated within the context of the Eucharist, contain a prayerful commendation of the dead into the hands of a merciful and gracious God, though this does not extend to a common practice of prayer for the dead beyond funerals.[33]

While the doctrine of purgatory is hardly at the top of the hierarchy of truths, the idea of some kind of purification before we enter into the presence of God in his majesty makes sense. Of course purgatory is not an anteroom to heaven, or in Ratzinger's words, "some kind of supra-worldly concentration camp."[34] An eschatological concept, it should not be imagined temporally or spatially. Ratzinger suggests that this purification involves not some *thing*, but rather an encounter with the transformative power of the Lord through which "a person becomes capable of Christ, capable of God and thus capable of unity with the whole communion of saints."[35] Thus, we should not think of this purification as something imposed by God; it should not be thought of as a preparation but as the result of our sinful condition in the presence of the holy. Coming before God's otherness is like trying to stare at the sun; we cannot do it. God's glory burns away the dross in us.

What is most attractive about Ratzinger's understanding of this process or moment of purification is that it is not the traditional, individualistic one. He reflects on our radically social nature, that our "own being is present in others as guilt or as grace," that to encounter Christ is to encounter his whole body: "I come face to face with my own guilt vis-à-vis the suffering members of that body as well as with the forgiving love which the body derives from Christ its Head."[36] In his encyclical on hope, *Spe Salvi*, Pope Benedict writes of this transforming encounter with Christ as savior and judge:

---

33. U.S. Lutheran–Roman Catholic Dialogue, "The Hope of Eternal Life" (2010), 64.

34. Ratzinger, *Eschatology*, 230.

35. Ibid.

36. Ibid., 232.

This encounter with him, as it burns us, transforms and frees us, allowing us to become truly ourselves. All that we build during our lives can prove to be mere straw, pure bluster, and it collapses. Yet in the pain of this encounter, when the impurity and sickness of our lives become evident to us, there lies salvation. His gaze, the touch of his heart heals us through an undeniably painful transformation "as through fire." But it is a blessed pain, in which the holy power of his love sears through us like a flame, enabling us to become totally ourselves and thus totally of God. (No. 47)

John Polkinghorne gives us a beautiful image, full of hope, in the context of the purging fire of judgment, though it might just as well apply to purgatory. He says that "just as a plant in a darkened cave will respond to the slightest glimmer of light that draws its growth in that direction, so we may hope that the slightest positive response to the light of God's presence will be enough to initiate in us the final work of salvation."[37]

How and when this happens remains a mystery. Does it happen after death or perhaps in the process of dying—a time often filled with memories, remorse, and hope—or perhaps even during this life? What seems to make most sense today is the idea that purgatory happens in that personal encounter with God that takes place at death.[38]

Heaven

How do we imagine heaven, perhaps the most popular eschatological symbol? It suggests a place where the just will one day be at home in God's presence. In the Old Testament, heaven (or "the heavens," as it often appears) means both the area above the earth and the place where God dwells. The New Testament speaks of heaven as the dwelling place and reward of the disciples of Jesus (Matt 5:12; 1 Thess 4:16-17). Paul stresses the incomprehensibility of our eternal destiny:

> What eye has not seen, and ear has not heard,
>   and what has not entered the human heart,
>   what God has prepared for those who love him." (1 Cor 2:9)

---

37. John Polkinghorne, *The God of Hope and the End of the World* (New Haven, CT, and London: Yale University Press, 2002), 132.

38. See Peter C. Phan, "Contemporary Context and Issues in Eschatology," *Theological Studies* 55 (1994): 519–20.

Other expressions include his words to "inherit the kingdom of God" (1 Cor 6:9; 15:50; Gal 5:21; cf. Eph 5:5) or more powerfully, to see God "face to face" (1 Cor 13:12). John's term "eternal life" (John 3:15, 36; 6:68; 12:50; 20:31) appears also in Paul (Rom 2:7; 6:23; 1 Tim 1:16). The historic creeds affirm our belief in "the life everlasting" (Apostles' Creed) and "the life of the world to come" (Nicene Creed).

Of course heaven is neither "up there" nor a place; to be in heaven means to be fully in God's presence. Walter Kasper expresses this beautifully when he says that heaven does not simply exist but comes into being "when the first created being is eschatologically and finally taken up by God. Heaven takes shape in the Resurrection and Exaltation of Christ."[39] Terence Nichols approaches heaven from both a theocentric and an anthropocentric perspective; heaven means the vision of God and the fulfillment of our deepest desires, that is, our hungers for love, understanding, beauty, freedom, goodness, and holiness, though he cautions that selfish desires, reflecting a life not yet transformed, cannot be fulfilled.[40] To this list we might add justice, when we think of all the innocent victims of history.

Ratzinger describes heaven as primarily a personal reality, "one that remains forever shaped by its historical origin in the paschal mystery of death and resurrection." One is "in heaven" to the degree that he or she is "in Christ," who as God and man makes space for human existence in the very existence of God.[41] Thus it is the fulfillment of our baptism, taking us into the communion of love of the Father, Son, and Spirit, which is the life of the Trinity.

At the same time, heaven is not just an individualistic reality; it has a social, ecclesiological dimension. "If heaven depends on being in Christ, then it must involve a co-being with all those who, together, constitute the body of Christ. Heaven is a stranger to isolation. It is the open society of the communion of saints, and in this way the fulfillment of all human communion."[42]

The *Eschaton*

If traditional eschatology has focused on the *eschata* and the destiny of the individual, today theologians are increasingly calling attention to

39. Walter Kasper, *Jesus the Christ*, (New York: Paulist, 1976), 152.
40. Nichols, *Death and Afterlife*, 166.
41. Ratzinger, *Eschatology*, 214.
42. Ibid., 235.

the *eschaton*. We have seen this dimension in the work of theologians such as Johann Baptist Metz, Jon Sobrino, Elizabeth Johnson, Peter Phan, and Terrence Tilley, all of whom stress the social dimension of the kingdom of God already breaking into the world through the ministry of Jesus. And while there is an element of judgment in the final coming of the *eschaton*, it is good news, the fullness of God's salvation, not just for suffering humanity but for creation itself.

The Victory of Justice

The resurrection of Jesus, the just man condemned to a shameful death, foreshadows the satisfaction of the deepest desires of humankind, that longing for vindication for so many throughout history who have suffered violence and death, the millions whose dignity has been scorned, whose rights have been abused, and whose lives have been taken. We can call to mind the genocides that have so scarred the twentieth century, from the tragedy of the Armenians as it opened, the estimated seven million who perished of starvation in Ukraine under Stalin, the Shoah or Holocaust with its five to six million Jewish victims, and the slaughters in Cambodia, to the innocents who died in the former Yugoslavia, in Rwanda, and in Sudan at its end. It is estimated that the Second World War claimed some twenty million victims, not to mention those who have died in the innumerable civil conflicts in Central America, Africa, and Asia. Then there are the countless innocent victims of violence, those persecuted and abused or those who perished from hunger, all those whose prayers seem to have gone unheard.

The fathers of the church recognized Jesus' solidarity with all who have suffered throughout history. Melito of Sardis, a late second-century bishop (d. ca. 180), expressed this beautifully in speaking of the mystery of Jesus' Passover, though the harshness of his language against the Jews is regrettable: "It was he who endured every kind of suffering in all those who foreshadowed him. In Abel he was slain, in Isaac bound, in Jacob exiled, in Joseph sold, in Moses exposed to die. He was sacrificed in the Passover lamb, persecuted in David, dishonored in the prophets."[43]

The resurrection shows that God's power conquers injustice in the age to come; it is evidence that the kingdom of God in its fullness will mean the victory of justice. For these victims of history, the words of the book of Revelation, using the image of the New Jerusalem coming down from

---

43. Melito of Sardis, "On the Pasch" 69; *Sources Chrétiennes* 123, 95–101.

heaven, are most appropriate: "Behold, God's dwelling is with the human race. He will dwell with them and they will be his people and God himself will always be with them [as their God]. He will wipe every tear from their eyes, and there shall be no more death or mourning, wailing or pain, [for] the old order has passed away" (Rev 21:3-4). In concluding his book on eschatology, Ratzinger writes, "the individual's salvation is whole and entire only when the salvation of the cosmos and all the elect has come to full fruition."[44] Thus the fullness of God's salvation also has a cosmic dimension.

The recovery of the eschatological concept of the kingdom or reign of God, with its social dimensions, has led to contemporary theologies of liberation in various forms. Those doing liberation theology, with its hope for justice, peace, and the transformation of society, hope for a liberation that embraces the oppressed and those who oppress them. Feminist theologians stress the embodied nature of our being, the risen body in its bodily, gendered integrity, and the collective destiny of the human race, along with a concern for the earth. This introduces a third theme, an ecological theology that not only looks forward to the inclusion of the cosmos in the process of salvation but also sees us partnering with God in helping creation grow and prosper. Finally, process theologians stress the dynamic nature of the afterlife and the relational, evolving nature not just of reality but also of the divine. Though Peter Phan cautions that an exclusive focus on inner-worldly realities, called "temporal messianism" by the International Theological Commission's document "Some Current Questions in Eschatology," risks a horizontalism, he finds these new theologies promising for the insights they offer.[45] Thus we are stewards, not masters, of creation.

A New Heaven and a New Earth

The New Testament is suggestive at best about the future of creation. Paul's understanding of the resurrection has both ecclesial and cosmic aspects; since Christ has indeed been raised, he is the "firstfruits" of those who have fallen asleep, and just as all die in Adam, so too in Christ all shall be brought to life. Christ will reign, putting his enemies under his feet, until the last enemy, death itself, is destroyed, and with all things

---

44. Ratzinger, *Eschatology*, 238.

45. See Phan, "Contemporary Context and Issues in Eschatology," 532–36; see International Theological Commission, Some Current Questions in Eschatology, *Irish Theological Quarterly* 58 (1992): 226; http://itq.sagepub.com/content/58/3/209.

subjected to Christ, the Son himself will be subjected to God so that God may be all in all (1 Cor 15:28). Then creation itself "will be set free from slavery to corruption and share in the freedom of the children of God" (Rom 8:21), a point stressed by the ITC document. Creation is groaning in labor pains (Rom 8:22). Thus Paul's argument envisions a return of humanity and creation itself to God through Christ. The theme is repeated in Colossians 1:15-20, which "interprets the full significance of the resurrection as an eschatological event that embraces the whole of creation from beginning to end."[46]

> He is the image of the invisible God,
>> the firstborn of all creation.
> For in him were created all things in heaven and on earth,
>> the visible and the invisible,
>> whether thrones or dominions or principalities or powers;
>> all things were created through him and for him.
> He is before all things,
>> and in him all things hold together. (Col 1:15-17)

The book of Revelation looks forward to a new heaven and a new earth, for "the former heaven and the former earth had passed away" (Rev 21:1; cf. 2 Pet 3:13). Ephesians speaks of God's plan set forth in Christ "to sum up all things in Christ, in heaven and on earth" (Eph 1:10). Nichols relates our own resurrection to a transfigured creation: "There would be no point in having a resurrected body if there were no resurrected environment."[47] Similarly, Anglican physicist and priest John Polkinghorne argues that the new creation will not be a radically new creation *ex nihilo* but a transformation of the old—a redeemed creation. But because matter, time, and space are linked according to the theory of general relativity, the new creation will also have matter, time, and space; it will be a temporal world whose character is everlasting.[48] Though his theological perspective is different, David Wilkinson, like Polkinghorne, stresses the centrality of the resurrection in eschatological

---

46. Michael L. Cook, *Trinitarian Christology* (New York: Paulist, 2010), 51.

47. Nichols, *Death and Afterlife*, 149; see also Lane, *Keeping Hope Alive*, 107.

48. Polkinghorne, *The God of Hope*, 116–17; cf. Ghislain Lafont, *A Theological Journey: Christian Faith and Human Salvation* (Collegeville, MN: Liturgical Press, 2007), 81.

thinking; he sees it as suggesting a transformative relation between creation and the new creation, mediated by the Spirit.[49]

We cannot imagine what this new creation will be like. It is far beyond
our experience. So we can continue to hope, drawing on the resources of
the biblical tradition, on our unpacking of the implications of the theology
of creation, the incarnation, and the resurrection, and on some of our most
visionary thinkers, as well as on our deepest desires for justice, reconciliation, peace, and communion. Brian Robinette suggests a point of
departure in the theology of creation: "Jewish monotheism defines a time
when evil was not; and it is just this imagination which necessitates the
eschatological anticipation of a time when evil will be no more. The cre-
ational monotheism of Judaism logically implies eschatology, and vice
versa."[50] In a more recent article, Robinette argues that for Christians the
resurrection of Jesus from the dead is the promise that God makes to
creation, calling to eschatological life what has succumbed to the nonbe-
ing of death.[51] From this perspective, the doctrine of *creatio ex nihilo* should
be seen as a doctrine of hope for creation, "a soteriologically motivated
doctrine that declares the penultimacy of evil, sin, and innocent suffering:
because they do not have the 'final' word—this is its 'eschatological vision'—neither are they 'original' or anterior to creation."[52]

Teilhard de Chardin builds his vision on the incarnation; he sees an
evolving, converging universe, matter itself becoming self-conscious,
moving toward personalization and communion, powered by love: "If
the world is convergent and if Christ occupies its centre, then the Chris-
togenesis of St. Paul and St. John is nothing else and nothing less than
the extension, both awaited and unhoped for, of that noogenesis in which
cosmogenesis—as regards our experience—culminates. Christ invests
himself organically with the very majesty of his creation."[53] Teilhard's
vision may be more poetic than scientific, but it is radically Christian,
rooted in the awareness that the divine word entered into space and time

49. David Wilkinson, *Christian Eschatology and the Physical Universe* (New York:
T. & T. Clark, 2010).

50. Brian D. Robinette, *Grammars of Resurrection* (New York: Crossroad, 2009),
359.

51. Brian D. Robinette, "The Difference Nothing Makes: *Creatio ex Nihilo*, Resurrection, and Divine Gratuity," *Theological Studies* 72 (2011): 545.

52. Ibid., 555.

53. Pierre Teilhard De Chardin, *The Phenomenon of Man* (New York: Harper and
Row, 1961), 297.

and history and became flesh. Building on Teilhard's worldview as well as on Scripture, Ilia Delio stresses that we meet Christ not just in the encounter of faith but at the heart of the evolutionary process; we meet him "in the divine, continual act of creation, redemption, and sanctification of the total universe. In him we discover the Absolute, the beginning and end of all unity in the cosmos."[54]

Karl Rahner has a similar vision. He seeks to develop his Christology within an evolutionary view of the world, though his starting point is different from that of Teilhard. His starting point is the fundamental unity of spirit and matter, by which he means that matter and spirit are not completely disparate realities but have more in common than they are different. Since human persons experience themselves as oriented toward the absoluteness of reality as such, with an orientation toward self-transcendence, Rahner sees no reason to deny that matter should have developed toward life and humanity. From this perspective, the incarnation appears as the necessary and permanent divinization of the world as a whole.[55]

> For there is no problem in understanding what is called creation as a partial moment in the process in which God becomes world, and in which God in fact freely expresses himself in his Logos which has become world and matter. We are entirely justified in understanding creation and Incarnation not as two disparate and juxtaposed acts of God "outwards" which have their origins in two separate initiatives of God. Rather in the world as it actually is we can understand creation and Incarnation as two movements and two phases of the one process of God's self-giving and self-expression, although it is an intrinsically differentiated process.[56]

Building on Rahner's evolutionary Christology, Hyun-Chul Cho argues that since the New Testament witnesses to Jesus' resurrection and total transformation, coming to exist in an utterly new way, the resurrection can be considered as the fulfillment of the incarnation just as the incarnation is the goal toward which the world is oriented; so "we can anticipate that all creatures in the world and the world itself will be transformed in a way analogous to Jesus' transformation in the

---

54. Ilia Delio, *Christ in Evolution* (Maryknoll, NY: Orbis, 2008), 132.
55. Rahner, *Foundations of Christian Faith*, 178–86.
56. Ibid., 197.

resurrection. Eschatologically transformed, creatures will exist in a totally new way, both in themselves and, therefore, in relation to one another and to God."[57]

Thomas Berry, a priest, historian of religion, and student of evolution who taught for many years at Fordham University, was another visionary thinker. Greatly influenced by Teilhard's vision, though he did not receive his thought uncritically, Berry recognizes the scientific and technological progress that Western civilization, with its roots in the biblical tradition, has achieved, but he also laments the high cost to our earth and its life systems that has been the result, with the extinction of hundreds of thousands of species, the disappearance of the great rain forests, and the poisoning of the planet as we have plundered the earth for its resources. Thus he sees an inherently religious dimension to the ecological movement. He calls for an intimacy with the earth, for an "eco-justice" in which social and ecological concerns are intertwined, going so far as to suggest that the ultimate sacred community could be the universe itself. Like Teilhard, he sees the sacred in the material, arguing that the story of the emergent universe should be told as a psychic-spiritual and physical process, not as a random physical process. He affirms the "anthropic principle," which holds that from the beginning the tendencies of the universe have pointed toward the emergence of the human. In the end he calls on the biblical teachings of Paul and John to suggest that God's plan for redemption and sanctification includes the world in all its beauty.[58]

David Power acknowledges that the horizon of our eschatological belief is challenged by science, that the vision of a new heaven and a new earth has to be reconciled with understanding that the universe will outlast human habitation on earth: "Yet we keep on believing that human destiny is intertwined with the destiny of the universe, and that Christ's Lordship, or our vision of the Cosmic Christ, embraces the whole of reality within the single love of the Creator God."[59]

The incarnation means that God in Christ has entered into solidarity with creation. Active in its origin, sustaining it throughout its marvelous

---

57. Hyun-Chul Cho, "Interconnectedness and Intrinsic Value as Ecological Principles of the World: An Appropriation of Karl Rahner's Evolutionary Christology," *Theological Studies* 70/3 (2009): 637.

58. Thomas Berry, *The Christian Future and the Fate of the Earth* (Maryknoll, NY: Orbis, 2009), 35–45.

59. David N. Power, "Worship and Ecology," *Worship* 84/4 (2010): 303.

development, drawing it through love rather than violence, God awaits its return in Christ. The resurrection of Jesus confirms that God's love is stronger than death, and it is the source of hope for our own resurrection. The resurrection is something that happens not to our souls but to our bodies. Walter Kasper says that "through Jesus' Resurrection and Exaltation a 'piece of the world' finally reached God and was finally accepted by God."[60] Perhaps that suggests that nothing good or beautiful will ever be lost. Eschatology is indeed the full flowering or completion of creation. Then indeed God will be all in all (cf. 1 Cor 15:28).

Conclusion

The individualism that is the stepchild of modernity transformed the Christian understanding of eschatology into a solitary notion of salvation. Called before the bar of God's judgment, each person would enter into bliss or be banished to the fiery realm, for conservative Protestants the fate of all those who had not accepted Jesus as Lord and Savior. At the same time, many Christians are more accustomed to thinking about their eschatological hope in terms of the immortality of the soul rather than on the basis of the basic Christian confession of the resurrection of the body, what Joseph Ratzinger calls "the central star in the firmament of Christian confession."[61]

What has been lost is the rich sense of the *eschaton*, the coming of God's kingdom in its fullness, the triumph of God's justice that would vindicate all those who suffered injustice or persecution, binding up their wounds, wiping the tears from their eyes, and raising them to life eternal with Christ. Creation itself would share in Christ's victory over sin and death; there would be a new heaven and a new earth, set free from corruption and slavery, subject finally to God, who would be all in all. Eschatology is the completion of creation; the theology of the one implies the other.

Still, each of us must one day face that transition from this world to the next that is called death, to be revealed in the pure light of truth for what we have become. The *eschata*, the last things, death and judgment, heaven and hell, are symbols for the completion of our personal stories. As Rahner says, the death of a Christian in the state of grace is different

---

60. Walter Kasper, *Jesus the Christ*, 152.
61. Ratzinger, *Eschatology*, 134.

from that of a sinner; because he or she lived in Christ, so also his or her dying was in Christ.[62] "Hell" is the state of those who, having closed themselves off from others and from God, are able to love only themselves and so cannot escape their self-chosen solitude. "Purgatory" symbolizes a final burning away of ego and self-centeredness in the blinding light of God's glory, rendering us transparent so that the true self might emerge. "Heaven" is the perfection of communion with others and with God that has long been part of one's personal story. In biblical terms, it means to see God face to face, to know fully even as we are known (1 Cor 13:12).

62. Rahner, *On the Theology of Death*, 75–77.

6

Eschatology and Liturgy

As we have seen, the early Christians gave expression to their eschatological hope in Christ's triumphant return when they gathered as a community of the saints on Sunday, the first day of the week, to celebrate the Eucharist. They called out in prayer, *Maranatha*, "Come, Lord Jesus," one of the church's oldest prayers, faced toward the east to await his return, and prayed for the coming of the kingdom in the Lord's Prayer.

The Eucharist as the meal of salvation has deep roots in Scripture. The image of the great banquet in the messianic age appears for the first time in the so-called Apocalypse of Isaiah (Isa 24:1–27:13), most probably a later addition to First Isaiah, which looks forward to the day of salvation, described in apocalyptic terms, when the Lord will punish the cosmic powers, the kings of the earth, and the wicked, destroying death, raising the dead to life, and taking away the guilt of his people. At its center appears the image of the great feast on Mount Zion that the Lord will prepare for all peoples:

> On this mountain the Lord of hosts
>   will provide for all peoples
> A feast of rich food and choice wines,
>   juicy, rich food and pure, choice wines.
> On this mountain he will destroy
>   the veil that veils all peoples,
> The web that is woven over all nations;
> He will destroy death forever.
> The Lord God will wipe away
>   the tears from all faces;
> The reproach of his people he will remove
>   from the whole earth; for the Lord has spoken. (Isa 25:6-8)

Some of these images reappear in the New Testament in the book of Revelation, which speaks of a new heaven and a new earth, the New Jerusalem coming down from heaven when God comes to dwell with the human race, wiping every tear from the eyes of the people, and there will be no more death or mourning or pain (Rev 21:1-4).

Jesus frequently appealed to this image of the messianic banquet in his preaching, saying that many would come from the east and the west to recline with Abraham, Isaac, and Jacob at the banquet in the kingdom of heaven (Matt 8:11; Luke 13:29). At times he imaged the eschatological banquet as a wedding feast (Matt 22:1-14; Luke 14:15-24). His tradition of table fellowship and the Last Supper were both signs of the kingdom. His practice of table fellowship was a sign of the kingdom's inclusiveness, welcoming tax collectors and sinners, a practice for which he received considerable criticism from the religious authorities. He was called "a glutton and a drunkard, a friend of tax collectors and sinners" (Matt 11:19; cf. Mark 2:16; cf. Luke 15:2).

At the Last Supper he gave a new meaning to this meal tradition, associating it not only with his death but also with the coming of the kingdom. In a verse judged by many critics to be authentic, he promised his disciples a renewed fellowship beyond his approaching death: "I tell you, from now on I shall not drink this fruit of the vine until the day when I drink it with you new in the kingdom of my Father" (Matt 26:29; cf. Luke 22:18; cf. Mark 14:25). Eschatological themes woven through the Last Supper accounts include the emphasis on memory, the new covenant in his blood (Luke 22:19-20; 1 Cor 11:24-25), drinking wine in the kingdom, and proclaiming the Lord's death until he comes again (1 Cor 11:26). The story of the miracle of the loaves in the gospels also echoes this theme of the eschatological banquet; the abundance left over, "twelve wicker baskets full of fragments" (Mark 6:43 and parallels), suggests an eschatological fullness. Thus, the Eucharist involves both memory and hope.

In this chapter we will consider liturgical time and memory, the relation between liturgy and social justice, rooted in the assembly's awareness of itself as the Body of Christ, and finally, we will make some suggestions toward the liturgical retrieval of the eschatological imagination.

Liturgical Time and Memory

In the opening chapter I stressed the role of memory in liturgy. Israel actualized its tradition through memory, especially through liturgical action, and in asking God to remember the covenant, the Israelites were calling on the Lord to come graciously into their present situation. Both the Jewish Passover supper and the church's Eucharist are memorials, ritual meals that call past events into the present, making present God's saving action through narrative and ritual. In celebrating the Seder supper or Passover Haggadah, Jews are instructed to tell and to remember the day of the Exodus.[1] "The Passover was enacted not simply as a remembrance of things past but as a present encounter with the power and reality of God's liberating hand."[2] Similarly, at the Eucharist, Christians share the bread and the cup "in memory" of Jesus (1 Cor 11:24-25; Luke 22:19). Narrative tells the story of the Lord's Passover of the homes of the Israelites or of Jesus' Last Supper with his disciples. Ritual acts the story out by eating the unleavened bread, the bitter herbs, and the roasted lamb or by sharing the bread broken and the cup poured out.

Eucharist and Temporality

The Eucharist integrates time and eternity in what we might call the three tenses of salvation history. Christ's redemptive life, death, and resurrection—his sacrifice—are remembered and made present (*anamnesis*) through narrative and ritual action, the thanksgiving narrative of the great eucharistic prayer (past). The assembly gives thanks for the gifts of creation, redemption, and eternal life and recognizes the presence of the risen Jesus in the eucharistic action; God's transformation of the world is already present in an initial way. By their communion (*koinōnia*) in the Body and Blood of Christ, those gathered are constituted as his body for the world (1 Cor 10:16-17). Christian faith is fundamentally communal (present). Finally, in proclaiming Christ's death, the community anticipates his coming again in glory (1 Cor 11:26). The Eucharist is food for the journey, anticipating the eternal life in which they already share (future; cf. John 6:54-56). Thus the Eucharist is essentially eschatological, proclaiming Christ's coming in glory, anticipating the fullness of his kingdom in his eucharistic presence, remembering his life for others—the "dangerous memory" of his passion, death, and resurrection—and promising salvation for all creation.

The power of memory to break the relentless cycle of time and give new direction and hope has been suggested by the philosopher Walter

---

1. Shlomo Riskin, *The Passover Haggadah* (New York: KTAV Publishing, 1983), 13.

2. Don E. Saliers, *Worship as Theology: Foretaste of Glory Divine* (Nashville: Abingdon, 1994), 53.

Benjamin (1892–1940) and developed theologically by Johann Baptist Metz. Benjamin argues that history is not closed but remains open. In spite of the tragedies that history continues to pile up, the memory of its victims can give us new hope, moving us to transform the present. Though a nonbeliever, Benjamin is willing to grant theology a role.[3]

Metz gives Benjamin's argument theological form. In his political theology, memory has a fundamental, theological importance as an expression of eschatological hope. If I can paraphrase Metz's words somewhat, the dangerous memory of Christ's passion, death, and resurrection shapes the mission of the church. Expressed in the church's dogma and informing its understanding of history, anthropology, and time, particularly through its "anamnetic solidarity" with the dead and the conquered, the dangerous memory of Jesus frees us from the grip of evolutionary or chronological time, interpreted as a history of triumph and conquest.[4] Interestingly, Joseph Ratzinger says something very similar. He argues that when Western thought lost sight of Christian theology's christological and trinitarian mystery, it retreated into a nontrinitarian monotheism that leaves eternity and time as "isolated opposites," and God is separated from human beings by an unbridgeable chasm.[5] Some contemporary Christian Christologies have also lost sight of the trinitarian mystery.

From a theological perspective, the memory of Christ's passion, death, and resurrection mediates between God's absolute revelation and the one who receives that revelation.[6] It is truly a message of hope, a message that in Dermot Lane's words "challenges the ongoing historical forces of darkness and evil in the world, reminding us prophetically that injustice and death do not have the final word and therefore history remains open and incomplete and unfinished 'until he comes again.'"[7]

---

3. For a summary of Benjamin's argument, see Helmut Peukert, *Science, Action, and Fundamental Theology* (Cambridge, MA: MIT Press, 1984), 206–10.

4. Johann Baptist Metz, *Faith in History and Society: Toward a Practical Fundamental Theology,* trans. David Smith (New York: Seabury, 1980), 184.

5. Joseph Ratzinger, *Feast of Faith* (San Francisco: Ignatius, 1986), 21–22. For a similar Augustian view, see Hans Boersma's chapter "Tradition as Sacramental Time" in his *Heavenly Participation: The Weaving of a Sacramental Tapestry* (Grand Rapids, MI: William B. Eerdmans, 2011), 120–36.

6. Metz, *Faith in History and Society*, 197.

7. Dermot A. Lane, *Keeping Hope Alive: Stirrings in Christian Theology* (New York: Paulist, 1996), 206.

Entering into the Paschal Mystery

In his study of Metz and Alexander Schmemann, Bruce Morrill stresses how narrative and ritual acts of remembrance precipitate moments of decision for those who take part in them, a remembrance that in the early church was most firmly established in the Eucharist.[8] The church's worship was focused not just on giving thanks to God by recalling Christ's paschal mystery but on calling the assembly to enter into it. Stressing the pervasiveness of memory, remembrance, and commemoration in the Christian life of faith, Morrill argues that "the Lord's Supper does not function in isolation from the rest of the Church's practices of proclamation, commemoration, and decisions for actions in the world," yet "the commemoration of Jesus' death and resurrection . . . is central to all other aspects of the praxis of faith—both mystical and political/ethical."[9] Joining in the eucharistic celebration incorporates us more fully into the paschal mystery into which we were baptized (cf. Rom 6:3-4).

Robert Daly asks, how do Christians offer sacrifice? How do they become ritually, sacramentally, and really present to the Christ event?

> They do this both by celebrating Eucharist together and, in an extension of that liturgical act, make that Eucharist real by living it out in their daily lives. In the eucharistic celebration, a Christian assembly with its duly appointed presider prays to the Father through the Son, asking the Father to send the Holy Spirit to transform the eucharistic gifts and, through that transformation, to continue to transform the eucharistic assembly into the Body of Christ.[10]

Incorporated into his self-offering, we become Christ's body for the world.

A Diminished Sacramental Practice

The World Council of Churches' 1982 text entitled *Baptism, Eucharist and Ministry* speaks of the Eucharist as the meal of the kingdom: "The eucharist opens up the vision of the divine rule of creation which was promised as the final renewal of creation, and as a foretaste of it. Signs of

---

8. Bruce T. Morrill, *Anamnesis as Dangerous Memory: Political and Liturgical Theology in Dialogue* (Collegeville, MN: Liturgical Press, 2000), 163–64.

9. Ibid., 166.

10. Robert J. Daly, "Eucharistic Origins: From the New Testament to the Liturgies of the Golden Age," *Theological Studies* 66 (2005): 17.

this renewal are present in the world wherever the grace of God is manifest and human beings work for justice, love and peace."[11] Unfortunately, this sense for the kingdom of God breaking in, so strong among the early Christians in what we have described as the eschatological imagination, has largely disappeared, as we have argued in this book.

In a study on the term "mystical body" (*corpus mysticum*), Henri De Lubac shows how the term originally referred to the sacramental body of the Lord, or what was more often called the "sacrament of the body" or "the mystery of the body," while "body of Christ" or "true body of Christ" (*verum corpus*) meant the church. But a shift took place after the controversy with Berengar (999–1088); rather than being used for the sacramental species, *corpus mysticum* was increasingly used for the church. As "mystical body" passed from eucharistic to ecclesial usage, an overly individualistic eucharistic piety developed,[12] though other factors played a role as well. Joseph Ratzinger acknowledges that this development led to a diminishment or loss of the eschatological dynamism and corporate character (the sense of the "we") of eucharistic faith, though he is not completely opposed to it, for deeper theological reflection on Christ's presence led to a spiritual deepening and adoration, which he argues is in no way opposed to communion.[13]

Regrettably, many Roman Catholics have narrowed the Eucharist to a celebration of Christ's sacramental presence, to an individualistic communion with him, while conservative Catholics talk about the "miracle of transubstantiation." There is little sense of the liturgy as drawing us into the paschal mystery of Christ's passion, death, resurrection, and ascension to glory. The current interest in the Latin Tridentine Mass or "Extraordinary Form" of the Eucharist and its accompanying paraphernalia in some sections of the Catholic community is focused more on solemn ritual and adoration than on retrieving the eucharistic experience of the early Christian communities; one senses a fascination with the otherworldly, the mysterious, the supernatural. While this suggests a hunger for transcendence, it is not at all clear that this is transcendence rightly understood.

---

11. World Council of Churches, *Baptism, Eucharist and Ministry* (Geneva: WCC, 1982), no. 22.

12. Henri de Lubac, *Corpus Mysticum* (Notre Dame: University of Notre Dame Press, 2006), 79–80, 256–59.

13. Joseph Ratzinger, *The Spirit of the Liturgy* (San Francisco: Ignatius, 2000), 87–90.

The liturgy should express the transcendent mystery of Christ's presence, and adoration of the Blessed Sacrament is an appropriate expression of Catholic eucharistic faith. But the current interest in exaggerated ritualism, hierarchy, cassocks, and searches in the sacristy storeroom for ancient vestments, let alone Pontifical High Masses with gloved celebrants and prelates in thirty foot long *cappa magnas* or trains of watered red silk, seems more nostalgic and antiquarian than genuinely liturgical. It is not at all evident that it will deepen the people's participation in the memory of Christ's passion and resurrection.

Still less will it bring them to a greater awareness of themselves as Christ's body for the world. All it does is heighten the divide between clergy and laity. It is the Catholic version of what Schmemann critiques in contemporary Orthodox piety, "religious feeling" instead of faith, which on the surface of church life "often appears as the most absolute, one-hundred-percent bulwark of genuine 'churchliness' and 'true Orthodox piety,'" manifesting itself in a deep attachment to rituals, customs, traditions—all the outward forms of church life.[14]

It is also true that contemporary Catholic liturgical practice too often overemphasizes the dimensions of celebration, hospitality, and community. In an article on liturgy and contemporary culture, Francis Mannion analyzes what he calls the "subjectification of reality," making the individual rather than institutions or traditions the source of meaning and value, including morality. Furthermore, he criticizes the "intimization of society" that places intimacy, personal closeness, warmth, and radical familiarity ahead of worship and the public ritual, which, he says, always involves not just friends but fellow citizens and strangers.[15] Joseph Ratzinger has offered a similar criticism; he objects to the current tendency to make the liturgy a spectacle or show, something "made" by the whole community.[16]

Protestant practice also suggests a loss of the eschatological dimension of the Eucharist. While the practice of open communion represents an effort to symbolize the inclusive character of the kingdom, Protestant theology and ritual has too often been curtailed or abbreviated. Luther-

---

14. Alexander Schmemann, *The Eucharist: Sacrament of the Kingdom* (Crestwood, NY: St. Vladimir's Seminary Press, 1988), 145.

15. M. Francis Mannion, "Liturgy and the Present Crisis of Culture," *Worship* 62 (1988): 98–123.

16. Joseph Ratzinger with Vitterio Messori, *The Ratzinger Report* (San Francisco: Ignatius, 1985), 126.

ans often view the Lord's Supper narrowly as a celebration of forgiveness, while for Presbyterians it is a fellowship meal or commemoration of the Last Supper. Too often the practice of proclaiming the church's great prayer of thanksgiving, with its narrative of the life, death, and resurrection of Jesus, has been lost. The service is reduced to the "gospel warrant" or words of institution. Without the eucharistic prayer or anaphora, there is little likelihood of the narrative of the paschal mystery transforming the thoughts and actions of the participants. For the majority of evangelical Protestants today, not coming from liturgical traditions, the central focus of Christian life is not the transformative entry into Christ's paschal mystery, calling the believer to compassionate service in memory of Jesus, witnessing to the coming of the reign of God, but an individualistic "getting saved."

The liturgy is not just a celebration of forgiveness or a fellowship meal, nor is it a narrow focus on the "supernatural" transformation of the bread and wine. The Eucharist is an act of memory and hope in which the transcendent becomes immanent in sacramental signs. We proclaim in thanksgiving God's saving action in Christ, recognizing the risen Jesus present in the breaking of the bread, and long for his return to bring the fullness of the kingdom. Lutheran liturgist Gordon Lathrop argues that participation in the eucharistic assembly is participation in Christian eschatology, symbolized by full inclusion as an anticipatory sign of the unity of the kingdom.[17] He urges the adoption of the *ordo* or ancient rule of prayer as a basis for unity between the churches.

Liturgy and Social Justice

Virgil Michel (1888–1938), a monk from Saint John's Abbey in Collegeville, Minnesota, largely responsible for the liturgical movement in the United States, was well aware of the transformative potential of the liturgy. Michel never ceased to emphasize the connection between liturgy and social justice. Early in his career he had the opportunity to study in Europe, visiting Maria Laach and Mont César, both centers of the liturgical renewal then flourishing, and bringing him under the influence of Dom Lambert Beauduin (1873–1960), who brought a new awareness of

---

17. Gordon W. Lathrop, *Holy People: A Liturgical Ecclesiology* (Minneapolis: Fortress, 2006), 44.

the relationship between liturgy and social concern to the liturgical movement in Belgium.

Shortly after his return to the States, Michel suffered a nervous breakdown, the result of spreading his energies too widely. To recuperate, he was assigned to work with the Chippewa people in Minnesota where he spent several years, gradually coming to a great admiration for the simplicity of their way of life and their sense of community. His experience there, as well as what he learned from his own personal struggles with ill health, was to shape the direction he was to give to the liturgical movement in the United States as he resumed his academic work at Collegeville.[18]

Michel was ahead of his time in objecting to what he saw as the individualistic and subjective stance of American Catholics: "As long as the Christian is in the habit of viewing his religious life from the subjectivist and individualist standpoint, he will be able to live his daily life in terms of the prudent individualism and subjectivism without any qualms of conscience."[19] He saw a renewed sense for liturgy, one that would incorporate worshipers into the mystical body, uniting them with Christ and with all those who share his life, as the best way to break down the barrier between the sacred and the secular in popular American culture. "He who lives the liturgy will in due time feel the mystical body idea developing in his mind and growing upon him, will come to realize that he is drinking at the very fountain of the true Christian spirit which is destined to reconstruct the Social Order."[20] For Michel, the liturgy, with its focus on the paschal mystery, is a powerful way to reinvigorate both the church's mission and the laity's share in living it out.

Unfortunately, as Pecklers notes, ordinary parishes found it difficult to realize this vision of social and cultural transformation so important to Michel and other liturgical reformers, and it has not really born fruit in the liturgical life of the postconciliar church,[21] in spite of efforts on the part of pastors and theologians to emphasize the connection between

---

18. See Keith F. Pecklers, *The Unread Vision: The Liturgical Movement in the United States of America; 1926–1955* (Collegeville, MN: Liturgical Press, 1998), 124–37.

19. Cited by Pecklers, *The Unread Vision*, 128.

20. Virgil Michel, "With our Readers," *Orate Fratres* 5 (1931): 431; cited by Pecklers, *The Unread Vision*, 133.

21. Pecklers, *The Unread Vision*, 137; see also M. Francis Mannion, "Liturgy and the Present Crisis of Culture," *Worship* 62 (1988): 101.

liturgy and social justice. For example, Pope John Paul II in his 2003 encyclical *Ecclesia de Eucharistia* emphasized this connection:

> A significant consequence of the eschatological tension inherent in the Eucharist is also the fact that it spurs us on our journey through history and plants a seed of living hope in our daily commitment to the work before us. Certainly the Christian vision leads to the expectation of "new heavens" and "a new earth" (*Rev* 21:1), but this increases, rather than lessens, *our sense of responsibility for the world today*. I wish to reaffirm this forcefully at the beginning of the new millennium, so that Christians will feel more obliged than ever not to neglect their duties as citizens in this world. Theirs is the task of contributing with the light of the Gospel to the building of a more human world, a world fully in harmony with God's plan (no. 20).

Retrieving the Eschatological Imagination

How can we reclaim something of that eschatological imagination so evident in the liturgical celebrations of the early Christians? How can our liturgies call our people to a deeper sense of themselves as the Body of Christ and to their own share in his paschal mystery? How can we offer new hope to those who are without hope, to the poor, the oppressed, and the victimized? How can we cultivate an eschatological imagination "which nurtures and empowers life in the midst of violence and contradictions, our own and others', in which we live"?[22]

The early Christians saw the liturgy as proclaiming Christ's victory over sin and death and recognized that the risen, glorified Christ was already present among them in the sacrament of the altar. His presence meant that the kingdom or fullness of salvation was already being realized, breaking into time and space in their gathering and sending them forth in his name. As Don Saliers says, in the Eucharist the *eschaton* is being realized and still is to come. "Gathering around the Lord's Table for the meal, distinctions of class and social standing are reordered."[23]

Occasionally we gain an insight into this transformative power of the Eucharist, giving us glimpses of the kingdom when we experience our-

---

22. James Alison, *Raising Abel: The Recovery of the Eschatological Imagination* (New York: Crossroad, 1996), 179.
23. Saliers, *Worship as Theology*, 60.

selves as an assembly united in celebration, one family, raising our voices together in song, listening to the Word, pouring out prayers of petition, joining in praise and thanksgiving, opening our hands and our hearts for the Body of Christ that binds up our wounds and makes us one. The late Cardinal Joseph Bernardin expressed this beautifully in speaking about the Eucharist:

> At this table we put aside every worldly separation based on culture, class, or other differences. Baptized, we no longer admit to distinctions based on age or sex or race or wealth. This communion is why all prejudice, all racism, all sexism, or deference to wealth and power must be banished from our parishes, our homes and our lives. This communion is why we will not call enemies those who are human beings like ourselves. This communion is why we will not commit the world's resources to an escalating arms race while the poor die. We cannot. Not when we have feasted here on the "body broken" and the "blood poured out" for the life of the world.[24]

But we have to come to the Eucharist expecting to give, not just to receive. How often do we hear, "I don't get anything out of it?" Often there is little personal investment. But when liturgy is well done, with good preaching that relates to peoples' lives and with a dialogue of prayer, praise, and song, there is a transformation, however subtle and nondramatic, that takes place over time.

Presider

The one who presides has a key role in giving tone and direction to the liturgy. If his opening remarks are chatty or conversational, telling jokes or announcing ball scores, or asking who is celebrating a birthday, there will be little sense that the assembly is entering into the presence of the holy. Certainly the language of "celebration" is overused. Objecting to the "talk-show host approach to Catholic worship," John Baldovin recommends that presiders not be allowed any ad lib remarks during the liturgy, except for the homily, announcements, and prayers of the faithful.[25]

24. Joseph Bernardin, *Guide for the Assembly* (Chicago: Liturgy Training Publications, 1997), 20.

25. John F. Baldovin, *Reforming the Liturgy: A Response to the Critics* (Collegeville, MN: Liturgical Press, 2008), 152.

While assemblies today may lack a strong eschatological imagination, eschatological themes are not absent from the liturgy. In fact they are woven throughout the prayers of the Mass. Using the new Roman Missal (2010), we find:

- Creed: "He will come again in glory / to judge the living and the dead / and his kingdom will have no end."

- The final lines of the Creed confess, "I look forward to the resurrection of the dead / and the life of the world to come. Amen."

- Preface: there are frequent references to Christ coming again in glory in the prefaces, particularly during the Advent season.

- *Benedictus*: the ancient verse "Blessed is he who comes in the name of the Lord. / Hosanna in the highest" is prayed at the end of the *Sanctus*.[26]

- Eucharistic prayers: the expectation of Christ's second coming is mentioned in the Third and Fourth Eucharistic Prayer, in the First Eucharistic Prayer for Reconciliation, and in the four new Eucharistic Prayers for Use in Masses for Various Needs.

- Eucharistic acclamations: two of the three acclamations end with the verse "until you come again."

- The Lord's Prayer includes a petition for the coming of the kingdom.

- *Libera nos*: in its penultimate verse the presider prays, "as we await the blessed hope / and the coming of our Savior, Jesus Christ.

The presider can refer to these verses in his preaching, calling attention to the eschatological hope they express and bringing into prayer and reflection the many victims of history that await the Lord's justice and vindication. As Bruce Morrill suggests from his reading of Metz, contemporary ecclesial communities might "need to be more explicit in their remembrance of those who are currently living in suffering, turmoil, or oppression."[27] Nor should it be presumed at the Mass for Christian

---

26. Out of a concern for more inclusive language, some say, "blessed is *the one* who comes," but this is to deprive this ancient verse of its all-important christological reference.

27. Morrill, *Anamnesis as Dangerous Memory*, 208.

Burial that the deceased are already in heaven.[28] We intercede at our liturgies for the suffering and the dead, that they might experience the fullness of God's salvation. These themes can also be appropriately brought into the homily. The readings at the end of the liturgical year just before Advent, when eschatological and apocalyptic themes are so prevalent, represent a rich invitation to address them.

Eucharistic Presence

We have seen how attention in the liturgy has been narrowly focused on the transformation of the bread and wine into the Body and Blood of Christ. The Second Vatican Council tried to address this, speaking of the multiple ways in which Christ is present in the church, while emphasizing his special presence in her liturgical celebrations: he is present in the person of the minister, in the sacraments, in his Word, when the church prays and sings, and "especially in the eucharistic species" (SC 7).

But Christ's eucharistic presence is not ordered primarily toward adoration but to the transformation of the assembly into the Body of Christ for the world (1 Cor 10:16-17). In part III of the *Summa Theologiae*, Aquinas gives three reasons for Christ's institution of the Eucharist: first, to remain with his own in the sacramental species; second, as a remembrance of his passion through which we are saved; and third, in a more personal explanation, Aquinas says that the last words of departing friends are deeply committed to memory, making the deepest impression and enkindling more affection.[29] Putting this into more contemporary language, David Power stresses the eschatological and ecclesial dimensions of the sacrament and its summons to participate in Christ's paschal mystery:

> What needs to be brought to the fore today is that it is by communion in the flesh and blood of Christ that the faithful come to share in the hope of his resurrection and in the gift of eternal life, for it is this that most tellingly transforms human life and gives hope in times of stress. A deep union with Christ himself in the eschatological gift of the Spirit is what is offered and promised, but it has to be guar-

---

28. Kevin W. Irwin, "Toward a New Liturgical Movement," *Origins* 40/46 (April 28, 2011): 749.

29. Thomas Aquinas, *Summa Theologiae* III, q. 73, a. 5.

anteed by a communion with him in his suffering through the way of discipleship on this earth.[30]

Similarly, Karl Rahner says that the "effect" of the Eucharist is not just personal participation in the life of Jesus for the individual; it also has an especially social and ecclesial effect, making God's salvific will present, tangible, and visible in that sign which is the church, the sign of the ultimate unity of all in the Spirit.[31] The grace of the sacrament (*res sacramenti*) is union with the Body of Christ.

Role of the Assembly

Vatican II's Constitution on the Sacred Liturgy, *Sacrosanctum Concilium*, calls for all the faithful to be led to "that full, conscious, and active part in liturgical celebrations which is demanded by the very nature of the liturgy" (SC 14), reminding pastors that they are to "ensure that the faithful take part fully aware of what they are doing, actively engaged in the rite and enriched by it" (SC 11). "To develop active participation, the people should be encouraged to take part by means of acclamations, responses, psalms, antiphons, hymns, as well as by actions, gestures and bodily attitudes. And at the proper time a reverent silence should be observed" (SC 30).

Joseph Ratzinger has long argued that what is central to the liturgy is not what we do, but rather the centrality of Christ and thus the action of God. For him, "active participation" (*actuosa participatio*) does not mean something external, with as many people as possible visibly engaged. "By the *actio* of the liturgy the sources mean the Eucharistic Prayer. The real liturgical action, the true liturgical act, is the *oratio*, the great prayer that forms the core of the Eucharistic celebration."[32] When the priest speaks with the "I" of the Lord, it is now God acting through Christ. "The elements of the earth are transubstantiated, pulled, so to speak, from their creaturely anchorage, grasped at the deepest ground of their being, and changed into the Body and Blood of the Lord. The New Heaven and the New Earth are anticipated." This is the great mystery into which we are drawn, praying that Christ's sacrifice becomes ours, conforming us to

---

30. David N. Power, *The Eucharistic Mystery: Revitalizing the Tradition* (New York: Crossroad, 1992), 294.

31. Karl Rahner, *Foundations of Christian Faith: An Introduction to the Idea of Christianity* (New York: Seabury, 1978), 426–27.

32. Joseph Ratzinger, *The Spirit of the Liturgy* (San Francisco: Ignatius, 2000), 171–72.

himself, being made into the true Body of Christ. This is the true action in the liturgy in which we are called to participate.[33]

Joseph Ratzinger / Pope Benedict XVI does not mean that the members of the assembly should be mere spectators. In his apostolic exhortation *Sacramentum Caritatis* (2007), written after his election to the Chair of Peter, he stresses that there should be no antithesis between the art of proper celebration (*ars celebrandi*) and the full, active, and fruitful participation of all the faithful (no. 38). Yet some misunderstandings have arisen as to the meaning of participation. It refers, he says, not to "mere external action" but rather to "a greater awareness of the mystery being celebrated and its relation to daily life" (no. 52). The commemorations of the living and the dead offer an opportunity for the members of the assembly to raise up to God those who suffer and who have suffered, all those who wait for God's justice, bringing them into the eucharistic prayer and into Christ's sacrifice.

The Eucharistic Prayer

Pope Benedict is correct of course. The great eucharistic prayer should draw the entire assembly into the mystery of Christ's sacrifice, the paschal mystery of his life, death, and resurrection, to a greater sense of themselves as Christ's body for the world, and to anticipation of his coming in glory. Unfortunately, the eucharistic prayer is a moment in the liturgy that too often renders the assembly largely passive. In the "Awakening Church" survey, Don Saliers raises the problem of minimal attentiveness to the eucharistic prayer.[34]

One problem concerns posture. In their study *The Postures of the Assembly during the Eucharistic Prayer* John Leonard and Nathan Mitchell argue that the earliest evidence indicates that during the eucharistic prayer Christians stood with arms outstretched, as is evidenced by the figure of the *orantes* in early Christian iconography. The Roman Canon, more or less fixed in the sixth century, refers to the *circumadstantes*. Beginning in the seventh and eight centuries, it became customary for those present to bow their heads while standing (*inclinantes*) from the beginning of the *Sanctus* to the end of the Canon. This position was still considered normative for the eucharistic prayer as late as the tenth and eleventh centuries and was attested to as late as Durandus at the end of

33. Ibid., 173.

34. Don E. Saliers, "Symbol in Liturgy, Liturgy as Symbol," in *The Awakening Church*, ed. Lawrence J. Madden (Collegeville, MN: Liturgical Press, 1992), 72.

the thirteenth century and even later.[35] The practice of standing during the liturgy remains the normative posture among the Orthodox.

The 1975 General Instruction of the Roman Missal (GIRM) provided for the people to kneel from after the eucharistic prayer to the Great Amen, and as some congregations began to stand during the eucharistic prayer, the United States Conference of Catholic Bishops ratified the GIRM norm in 2003. Some liturgists object that this introduces an unfortunate difference in status between presider and assembly, diminishing the sense that the whole assembly joins in giving thanks. It is interesting to note that the fathers at the Council of Nicaea (325) added canon 20, forbidding the novel practice of kneeling during the eucharistic prayer. Ratzinger's *Spirit of the Liturgy* gives a long defense of the practice of kneeling during the liturgy, grounding it in Scripture, explaining canon 20 as a special privilege during Eastertide.[36] He does not mention the reference in the Roman Canon to the *omnium circumstantium*, "all those standing around" the altar.

Some propose that the eucharistic prayer be prayed by the assembly. But this would be a significant departure from the tradition. The practice of the presider "giving thanks" at the liturgy is an ancient one, going back at least as far as Justin Martyr (103–165). Singing or chanting the eucharistic prayer often brings about a greater attentiveness on the part of the assembly. And other ways might be tried to give the assembly a more active participation—beyond appealing to their intentionality, perhaps by adding some additional acclamations, spoken or sung, or even reclaiming the ancient prayer "Come, Lord Jesus." Or the verse that early in the church's liturgy replaced *Maranatha*, "Blessed is he who comes in the name of the Lord," might be used instead.

Not all our eucharistic prayers give expression to eschatological hope as clearly as they might. Bruce Morrill suggests that "there be in the epiclesis-intercession movements of the prayers a strong measure of the language and images of the taste, pledge, or promise of the fulfillment of God's reign, the heavenly banquet, the peaceable kingdom. Engagement in the language-event of such imagery could heighten the sense of imperative (and hope)

---

35. John K. Leonard and Nathan D. Mitchell, *The Postures of the Assembly during the Eucharistic Prayer* (Chicago: Liturgy Training Publications, 1994), 64–66; in his introduction to the book, John Baldovin notes that it is not without reason that the Orthodox have been characterized as "the church standing," Roman Catholics as "the church kneeling," and Protestants as "the church sitting" (3).

36. Ratzinger, *The Spirit of the Liturgy*, 184–97 at 195.

for engaging in the praxis of gospel faith (kenotic service) in the world."[37] He notes that the Roman Canon "failed to associate the Eucharistic anamnesis with Christ's second coming and the final judgment." The eschatological hope of the church is much more beautifully expressed in the eucharistic prayer of the Second Mass of Reconciliation:

> Bring us to share with them the unending banquet of unity
> in a new heaven and a new earth,
> where the fullness of your peace will shine forth.[38]

Conclusion

The image of the great messianic banquet as a sign of salvation has its origins in the Old Testament and appears frequently in Jesus' preaching about the kingdom of God. It found expression in his practice of table fellowship, and eschatological themes are woven throughout the tradition of the Last Supper. The Eucharist is the meal of the kingdom.

If the modern liturgical movement has led to a renewal of eucharistic practice in many churches, rarely has the sense been recovered for the inbreaking of the kingdom, what we have called the eschatological imagination. Liturgical scholarship has reclaimed the connection between liturgy and social justice and has emphasized the power of memory to link the church of today with all the victims of history, reminding the congregation that evil does not have the final word. But this scholarship has yet to reclaim an eschatological dimension for our liturgical practice.

Too often Catholics focus on celebration, hospitality, and community or reduce their eucharistic theology to a fascination with the change of the elements, the "Real Presence," while Protestants have abridged their liturgical practice or unduly narrowed their theological focus. Many Protestant churches, no longer liturgical, celebrate the Eucharist only infrequently. If our presence at the liturgy does not affect how we live our daily lives, we have not truly been nourished by our participation.

We should not expect some dramatic empowerment when we take part in the Eucharist. Grace builds on nature; it does not eradicate it. But when the liturgy is done well, with presiders drawing the assembly into the presence of the holy, and the assembly is united in prayer, praise,

---

37. Morrill, *Anamnesis as Dangerous Memory*, 204.
38. Ibid., 207.

and contemplation of Christ's sacrifice, the liturgy can be truly transformative. At the table we become one family. The future that God has in store for us is already breaking into the present. The risen Christ unites himself to us, gathering us in his name, incorporating us into his paschal mystery, filling us with his Spirit, and making us his body for the world.

7

Eschatology, Christology, and Church

Throughout this book we have sought to recover the hope and expectation of the early Christians, particularly in their liturgical celebrations, for Christ's coming in glory, bringing the fullness of the kingdom. Then, according to the biblical vision, the long-awaited messianic age would be realized in its completeness, with justice for the poor and afflicted, freedom for captives, peace, the resurrection of the dead, and the renewal of creation. This was the fullness of the kingdom proclaimed by Jesus during his historical ministry, symbolized, and realized in his resurrection.

As we draw this work to a close, we need to gather together some of the themes we have been pursuing. First, we need to reflect on the imaginative language of Christian hope, in order to better understand the eschatological dimensions of Christian faith. Then, we will return to the subjects of Christology, the church, and its mission in light of some of the new developments in theology we have considered in the course of this study. Finally, we will try to summarize our conclusions.

From Imagination to Understanding

Throughout this work we have been examining a number of eschatological symbols and concepts in the effort to understand the fullness of our salvation. Some of them are images, ideas imaginatively conceived, such as heaven and hell, purgatory, the last judgment, the risen body, and the second coming of Christ. Others, like the soul, are more properly philosophical concepts, less easily imagined. To better understand them, we need to reflect briefly on the nature of theological language.

Theology always describes the efforts of the believing community to bring its faith and religious experience to expression in stories, analogies, language, and concepts, but as I have argued elsewhere, our theological language, including our doctrines, always remains a second-order language, removed by one or more levels from the experience it seeks to express.[1] Each religious symbol—whether story or image—contains a surplus of meaning. We have to be comfortable moving from the more literal interpretation of a symbol, through its imaginative content, to the intelligibility each attempts to express; image and intelligibility are not necessarily identical. We cannot reduce the meaning of these symbols to their imaginative contents, but neither should their fundamental intelligibilities be contradicted. Nor can we forget that much of our eschatological hope remains mystery, as we pointed out at the beginning.

Intelligent Christian faith does not require of us a biblical literalism. For example, trying to retrieve the relationship between Eucharist and eschatology in the early church does not mean that we are committing ourselves to a literalistic view of the Parousia, as though Jesus were going to descend some afternoon with a blare of trumpets into the midst of the rush hour traffic on the San Diego Freeway. Nor do we need to turn our altars toward the east to greet his advent.

We do not pray like the early Christians, but belief in the Second Coming means at least that Christ in some way will come in God's own time to gather his own, bringing the kingdom in its fullness and creation to its completion. While we cannot imagine how this will happen, understanding that our bodies and creation itself will in some way share in the fullness of salvation means that both should be treated with a greater reverence and respect.

We tried to understand purgatory as the purification that takes place after death, or in the process of dying, or perhaps even in this life, when we are confronted with God's uncreated light that will reveal each of us for the persons we have become, letting our true selves emerge. It is not an anteroom to heaven. Nor is hell a place; it is the state of those who have closed themselves off from sustaining relationships with others and with God. Similarly, heaven is to be in communion with love eternal. It is "the fulfillment and consummation of choices we have made in this

---

1. See Thomas P. Rausch, *I Believe in God: Reflections on the Apostles' Creed* (Collegeville, MN: Liturgical Press, 2008), 18–23.

life, for or against God."[2] While heaven is difficult to imagine, its meaning is something that we not only can grasp but also long for from the depths of our being.

We can imagine the Last Judgment as a great assembly before a royal or triumphant Christ, as it has so often been portrayed in Christian art. But what the concept suggests is that our eternal destiny will be shaped by the ways we have responded to God's abundant grace as well as by the good or evil we have done. The idea of the Last Judgment affirms that the way we have lived our lives is not without significance and that evil will not have the final word. Most of all, the resurrection of Jesus is hope not just for the individual but foreshadows the victory of justice for all who have suffered unjustly. We look forward to that communion of love and life that is the Body of Christ, reunited with all those who have shaped our lives and who in turn we have helped shape. And creation itself, set free from corruption and failure and death, will find its completion in God who will be all in all (1 Cor 15:28).

Christology

The emphasis in recent years on the historical Jesus in christological scholarship has contributed greatly to a deeper understanding of Jesus and his ministry, his proclamation of the kingdom of God, and the social implications of his Gospel. There have been gains as well as some losses from this new approach.

Christ and the Kingdom

Positively, the rediscovery of the centrality of the kingdom or reign of God has led to a deeper understanding of Christian discipleship and to a new appreciation that salvation cannot be reduced to an individualistic sense of being "saved" and going to heaven. The reign of God has an inescapably social, even political character, as we have seen in the works of theologians such as Johann Baptist Metz, Jon Sobrino, Elizabeth Johnson, Terrence Tilley, and Dermot Lane—and to the list we could add Ignacio Ellacuría, who so influenced Sobrino. Ellacuría speaks of how the *Spiritual Exercises* of Ignatius of Loyola "historicize" the Word of God,

---

2. Terence Nichols, *Death and Afterlife: A Theological Introduction* (Grand Rapids, MI: Brazos, 2010), 54.

interweaving one's own personal history with the broader world history in which it is embedded and with the history of God's salvific work in the world, manifested definitively in Jesus. "The goal is the praxis of discipleship."[3] Even conservative Protestants are asking questions today about whether the Gospel is centered on Paul or on Jesus; is it about justification by faith or the kingdom of God?[4] Of course, the contrast represents a false dilemma; the Gospel includes both, even if justification by faith does not exclude the importance of discipleship, the imitation of Christ in his paschal mystery, and our obligation to witness to the kingdom of God.

The rediscovery of the kingdom has also led to a deeper understanding of Christology itself. Theologians like Metz, Sobrino, and Tilley have emphasized that the key to Christology is praxis. For Metz, Christianity is a messianic praxis of discipleship; he argues that "every Christology is subject to the primacy of praxis."[5] In Bruce Morrill's words, "Metz's christological thesis is that one only knows Christ by imitating him."[6] Similarly, for Tilley, being a disciple means living in and living out the reign of God by engaging in the reconciling practices that characterized Jesus' movement.[7] Doctrine is secondary. Jon Sobrino also places the christological priority on praxis, challenging Christians to take the crucified peoples of the world down from the cross.[8]

3. J. Matthew Ashley, "Contemplation in the Action of Justice: Ignacio Ellacuría and Ignatian Spirituality," in *Love that Produces Hope: The Thought of Ignacio Ellacuría*," ed. Kevin F. Burke and Robert Lassalle-Klein (Collegeville, MN: Liturgical Press, 2006), 147–48.

4. See Scot McKnight, "Jesus or Paul," *Christianity Today* 54/12 (December 2010): 25–29.

5. Johann Baptist Metz, *Followers of Christ: Perspectives on Religious Life* (New York: Paulist, 1978), 40.

6. Bruce T. Morrill, *Anamnesis as Dangerous Memory: Political and Liturgical Theology in Dialogue* (Collegeville, MN: Liturgical Press, 2000), 34.

7. Terrence W. Tilley, *The Disciples' Jesus: Christology as Reconciling Practice* (Maryknoll, NY: Orbis, 2008), 252; Pope John Paul II says something similar in his encyclical *Redemptoris Missio*: "The kingdom aims at transforming human relationships; it grows gradually as people slowly learn to love, forgive and serve one another" (no. 15).

8. Jon Sobrino, *Christ the Liberator: A View from the Victims* (Maryknoll, NY: Orbis, 2001), 47; see also Robert LaSalle-Klein, "Jesus of Galilee and the Crucified People: The Contextual Christology of Jon Sobrino and Ignacio Ellacuría," *Theological Studies* 70 (2009): 347–76.

There is a universal dimension to the kingdom of God, as Pope John Paul II emphasized; it is not identified exclusively with the church. In his 1990 encyclical, *Redemptoris Missio*, the pope wrote:

> The kingdom is the concern of everyone: individuals, society, and the world. Working for the kingdom means acknowledging and promoting God's activity, which is present in human history and transforms it. Building the kingdom means working for liberation from evil in all its forms. In a word, the kingdom of God is the manifestation and the realization of God's plan of salvation in all its fullness. (No. 15)

And while the church serves the kingdom by spreading "gospel values" throughout the world, the reality of the kingdom can also be found among peoples everywhere, to the extent that they live those gospel values and are open to the working of the Spirit (no. 20). Jacques Dupuis argues that those who belong to other religious traditions perceive God's call through their own religious traditions and belong to the reign of God, even without being conscious of it. Along with Christians, they "build together the Reign of God whenever they commit themselves by common accord to the cause of human rights, and whenever they work for the integral liberation of each and every human person, but especially of the poor and the oppressed," and by promoting religious and spiritual values.[9] Thus, this new emphasis on the kingdom of God enables different religious traditions to find common ground.

All this is for the good. Christian life cannot be separated from a Christian discipleship that challenges all to witness to the reign of God; nor can the concept of the kingdom be stripped of its social, "political" meaning. When he speaks of a political theology, Metz does not mean a politics of parties, policies, and programs. Still less does he intend a purely technical administration, an old-style decision politics, or a Machiavellianism:

> What we need in the long run is a new form of political life and new political structures. Only when that arrives will there be any humane cultures at all in the future. In this sense, "politics" is actually the new name for culture and in this sense, too, any theology which tries

---

9. Jacques Dupuis, *Christianity and the Religions: From Confrontation to Dialogue* (Maryknoll, NY: Orbis, 2003), 202; see his chapter, "The Reign of God, the Church, and the Religions," 195–217.

> to reflect on Christian traditions in the context of world problems
> and to bring about the process of transference between the kingdom
> of God and society is a "political theology."[10]

The apocalyptic eschatology of the gospels is not simply otherworldly
or spiritual; it involves the real world and thus life in society (politics).
As Tilley says, ignoring the political aspects of reconciliation would be
to deny that reconciliation should permeate all the spaces in which we
live.[11]

Pope Benedict XVI, both before and after his election to the Chair of
Peter, has objected to political and liberation theologies for ignoring Jesus
as God's presence, active in history in a new way. He argues that a regnocentric approach to Christian faith reduces the kingdom to a secular-
utopian idea that makes God no longer necessary.[12] Though he may
need to acknowledge more clearly the social and political dimensions
of Jesus' proclamation of the kingdom, his point is a valid one. Pope John
Paul II said something similar in *Redemptoris Missio*; while he recognized
that there are positive aspects to a "kingdom-centered" approach, he
also cautioned that the kingdom cannot be detached from either Christ
or the church (nos. 17–18). The church's mission cannot be reduced to
the social.

But if Benedict, in his concern to safeguard the primacy of grace and
the divine initiative, seems reluctant to give expression to the social and
political implications of Jesus' preaching, others run the risk of collapsing
Christology and soteriology into ethics. There is a tension here that needs
to be kept in careful balance. Recent christological scholarship has given
us a much clearer understanding of Jesus' ministry, his concern for the
poor and the marginalized, especially evident in Luke and Matthew, and
the involvement of his disciples in witnessing to God's reign. Echoing
the messianic vision of justice for the poor, comfort for those who mourn,
and liberty for captives, Jesus declares the poor, the suffering, those who
hunger and thirst for justice blessed (Matt 5:3-10; Luke 6:20-21) and tells
us that we will be judged on the basis of how we care for the last and
the least (Matt 25:31-46). Thus Jesus reveals that a relationship with God
requires a proper relationship with other human beings, one based on

---

10. Johann Baptist Metz, *Faith in History and Society: Toward a Practical Fundamental Theology*, trans. David Smith (New York: Seabury, 1980), 102.

11. Tilley, *The Disciples' Jesus*, 242–48 at 244.

12. Pope Benedict XVI, *Jesus of Nazareth* (New York: Doubleday, 2007), 53–55.

justice, love, and service. Tilley's work, stressing practices of reconciliation, broadly understood, is helpful here.

In his encyclical on hope, *Spe Salvi* (2007), Pope Benedict carefully distinguishes between Christian hope and hope that is merely faith in progress (nos. 16–23). He insists that secular hope, for example for the improvement of the world, cannot be the sufficient content of our hope. Dominic Doyle argues that Benedict is correct in urging their radical discontinuity, in light of the traumas experienced in twentieth-century Europe when the distinction between eschatological hope and political hope collapsed, opening the way to totalitarian ideologies. He quotes from Benedict's book on eschatology, which states that "the setting asunder of eschatology and politics is one of the fundamental tasks of Christian theology."[13] But Doyle argues from Aquinas to suggest that there is a unity between secular and eschatological hopes: "not only do our secular hopes participate in eschatological hopes, but more fundamentally we only participate in eschatological hope in and through our secular hopes and actions."[14] One illustration of this is Aquinas's treatment of the Beatitudes, which he sees as acts flowing from the theological virtues and the gifts of the Holy Spirit, for being merciful, striving for justice, making peace, and so on, merit a particular reward.[15]

Therefore, rather than stressing the contrast between secular hope and eschatological hope, Doyle wants to talk about how secular hope can bring one to participate in God's power and mercy. "As a result, the person is empowered to become an agent of God's justice and mercy in the world. Indeed, Matthew 25 presents the criteria of judgment for eschatological worthiness as precisely the commitment to such secular concerns of justice and mercy. For all the undeniable contrast between secular and eschatological hopes, there exists a deeper analogical participation."[16] Dupuis puts it this way: "In the building of the Kingdom the two dimensions, human and religious, are inseparable. Indeed, the former is the sign of the latter."[17]

---

13. Dominic Doyle, "*Spe Salvi* on Eschatological and Secular Hope: A Thomistic Critique of an Augustinian Encyclical," *Theological Studies* 71/2 (2010): 358; see Joseph Ratzinger, *Eschatology: Death and Eternal Life*, 2nd ed., trans. Michael Waldstein (Washington, DC: Catholic University of America Press, 1988), 59.

14. Doyle, "*Spe Salvi* on Eschatological and Secular Hope," 370.

15. Ibid., 374.

16. Ibid., 379.

17. Dupuis, *Christianity and the Religions*, 202.

But Benedict is correct in warning against interpreting the Gospel as an argument for radical social change. Jesus' absolute renunciation of violence, even when his proclamation of the kingdom led to his own death, was distinctive of his ministry. In *Spe Salvi*, Benedict says that "Christianity did not bring a message of social revolution like that of the ill-fated Spartacus, whose struggle led to so much bloodshed" (no. 4). His *Jesus of Nazareth* is eloquent testimony to the fact that the mission of Jesus cannot be separated from his person, for Jesus is the kingdom of God in person.

Early High Christology

Some contemporary Christologies, motivated at least in part by a desire for dialogue with other religions, are unable to acknowledge Jesus' oneness with the Father or his preexistence. Constructed entirely "from below," based exclusively on the historical Jesus, they tend to treat Scripture as a history of primitive Christianity rather than an inspired text. A commitment to interreligious dialogue or to dialogue with a postmodern world does not require a redefinition of Christian faith in a way that is contrary to the Christian tradition, as we will argue below. We would not expect our dialogue partners to water down their own religious beliefs for the sake of dialogue. Such an approach is neither necessary nor honest.

Some of these contemporary Christologies need to pay greater attention to the faith experience of the earliest Christian communities. If they do not, they run the risk of too easily separating the Jesus of Christian faith from the biblical tradition as well as from his cosmic, eschatological role. Separated from his mission, he is no longer the universal savior or bringer of salvation but one among other mediators disclosing the way to God, although a normative one for Christians. Nor is he the unique incarnation of the Word, the one whose resurrection ushered in the *eschaton*, at least in an initial way.

While it has long been the position of much of mainstream christological scholarship that high Christology proclaiming the preexistence of Jesus developed late in the tradition, with some arguing that it was shaped by Hellenistic influences, a number of recent developments make that position increasingly difficult to maintain. They include, first, the fact that Jesus was addressed as *Kyrios* or Lord by the early Christian communities even before Paul; second, that Jesus was the object of worship from very early in the Christian movement; and third, evidence that preexistence theology is present in Pauline Christianity or even earlier.

Especially significant is the work of Larry Hurtado on Jesus being the recipient of devotion and his being associated with God from very early in the Christian movement (ca. 30–50 CE).[18] Like others, Hurtado points out that the Greek *kyrios*, which among Greek-speaking Jews was a substitute for the divine name, was also used as a title for Jesus. In the Greek of the time, *kyrios* was used as a honorific form of address, like "master" or "sir," to one of superior status. But it was also used as a form of address to gods or to God. The same ambiguity is evident today in the Spanish *Señor* and German *Herr*, used both as a polite form of address and as a divine title.

Hurtado argues that the Christian use of the term goes back to the earliest circles of Jewish Christians; Jews at this time avoided pronouncing the Hebrew name of God, Yahweh, out of reverence, using various substitutes such as the Hebrew *Adonai* or the Aramaic *MarYah*, found in the Qumran texts, both meaning Lord. Among Greek-speaking Jews, it seems to have been common to use *kyrios* as a substitute for the divine name Yahweh. The fact that Paul can use the invocation *Maranatha*, "Our Lord, come," in Aramaic without translating it for his largely Greek-speaking congregation is evidence that "Lord" was used in reference to Jesus in Aramaic- and Greek-speaking Christian circles even before Paul's time. Similarly, he uses another Aramaic name, *Abba*, in his letters without translating it.[19]

Hurtado shows how Paul sometimes uses *kyrios* in reference to God both in cases where he is citing the Old Testament (Rom 4:8; 9:28-29; 10:16; 11:34) and in other contexts without a direct Old Testament equivalent (Rom 11:3; 12:19; 1 Cor 12:21), showing that *kyrios* substituted for God's name. But most often he uses *kyrios* as a title for Jesus, about 180 times in the undisputed letters. Sometimes these are in Old Testament passages Paul applies to Jesus, sometimes in similar passages that are ambiguous (Rom 14:11; 1 Cor 2:16); some are passages directly associating Jesus with God, others are acclamations of Jesus as Lord in early Christian worship (1 Cor 8:5-6; 12:3; Rom 10:9-10; Phil 2:9-11), as well as

18. Larry W. Hurtado, *Lord Jesus Christ: Devotion to Jesus in Earliest Christianity* (Grand Rapids, MI: William B. Eerdmans, 2003), 2; see also Carl Judson Davis, *The Name and Way of the Lord: Old Testament Themes and New Testament Christology* (Sheffield: Sheffield Academic Press, 1996).

19. Hurtado, *Lord Jesus Christ*, 108–11; see also Joseph A. Fitzmyer, "*Kyrios* and *Maranatha* and their Aramaic Background," in *To Advance the Gospel: New Testament Studies* (New York: Crossroad, 1981), 222.

about 170 cases where *kyrios* is used of Jesus in formulaic expressions, many of them from worship settings. Most frequently, *kyrios* is used in the absolute sense (with the definite article), about one hundred times in the undisputed letters, to designate Jesus simply as "the Lord" (*ho Kyrios*; e.g., Rom 14:6, 8, 11, 12, 13; 1 Cor 3:5; 4:4-5). In these cases it is clear that for Paul and his intended readers, " 'the Lord' is sufficient and no further identifying words are needed," as it was familiar from Hebrew (*Adonai*) and Aramaic (*MarYah*) references to God.[20]

Early Christian worship offers more evidence. Hurtado points to a "binitarian pattern" of devotion and worship that appeared in Pauline Christianity "astonishingly early," showing Christ as the "recipient of devotion with God and in ways that can be likened only to the worship of a deity."[21] To illustrate his point, he details a pattern of devotional practices that show Jesus as the recipient of unprecedented cultic devotion—not in private acts of individuals but in corporate liturgical gatherings, which can only be understood as the cultic worship of Jesus. This pattern of devotion includes prayer in which God and Jesus are addressed and invoked together (1 Thess 3:11-13; 2 Thess 2:16-17; 3:5), benedictions invoking God and Christ together (Rom 16:20; 1 Cor 16:23), and prayers addressed to Jesus (2 Cor 12:8-9; cf. Acts 7:59-60), including the *Maranatha*, apparently pre-Pauline, so familiar in liturgy that it needed no introduction or translation. Other examples include confessing "Jesus is Lord" (Rom 10:9-13; 1 Cor 12:3; Phil 2:10-11), as we have seen. The early Christians also baptized in Jesus' name; gathered for the Lord's Supper or Eucharist, associating the bread and wine of the meal with his redemptive death but honoring him not as a dead hero but as a living and reigning Lord; and sung christological songs or hymns (Phil 2:6-11; Col 1:15-20; John 1:1-18; Eph 5:14; 1 Tim 3:16), again some of them possibly pre-Pauline, in their worship.[22]

It is also true that an increasing number of scholars are coming to recognize evidence of preexistence Christology not as a late New Testament development but appearing as early as the pre-Pauline hymn in Philippians 2:6-11.[23] Reflective of Wisdom theology, this hymn speaks

---

20. Hurtado, *Lord Jesus Christ*, 114.

21. Ibid., 135.

22. Ibid., 137–49.

23. Tilley, *The Disciples' Jesus*, 111; see also Hurtado, *Lord Jesus Christ*, 118; Roger Haight acknowledges that reading this text as a descent Christology is gaining wider acceptance; see *Jesus Symbol of God* (Maryknoll, NY: Orbis, 1999), 169.

of Jesus as being "in the form of God," emptying himself and taking on the form of a slave. Furthermore, the hymn goes on to say that "every knee should bend, / of those in heaven and on earth and under the earth, / and every tongue confess that / Jesus Christ is Lord, / to the glory of God the Father" (Phil 2:10-11), invoking the three levels of the universe. In his study of the trinitarian implications of Christology, Michael Cook argues that while the hymn invokes the strict monotheistic faith of Isaiah 45:23, "it would be hard to find a more strongly worded, concrete expression of Jesus' divinity. He is the object of cosmic worship that includes heaven, earth, and the netherworld."[24]

A passage in 2 Corinthians 8:9 speaks of an exchange similar to the one in Philippians 2: Jesus Christ for your sake "became poor although he was rich, so that by his poverty you might become rich."[25] Paul also recognizes "the one Lord, Jesus Christ" as having a role in creation (1 Cor. 8: 6; cf. Col 1:15-16). These passages also reflect wisdom theology. Indeed for Paul, creation and redemption are joined, as we have suggested earlier; "Jesus' agency in creation corresponds to his central role in redemption (1 Cor 8:6), expressing his unique significance and the unity of divine purpose in creation and redemption."[26] This is a theme that would be developed later in the Fourth Gospel.

Christ's Eschatological Role

Paul's expectation of the imminent Parousia is evident in his early letters—for example, in his vision of the rapture (1 Thess 4:13-17). Later letters put greater stress on the resurrection, but for Paul, the end of the ages has already come (1 Cor 10:11), and we have the gift of the Spirit as the "firstfruits" (Rom 8:23) or a "first installment" (2 Cor 1:22; 5:5). Christ is the last or new Adam, the "firstfruits" of the resurrection of the dead to whom everything will be subjected, so that God may be all in all (1 Cor 15:21-28). Paul presents Christ Jesus as the wisdom of God (1 Cor 1:25), hidden for the ages but now manifest (Rom 16:25-26; cf. 1 Cor 2:7; cf. Col 1:26). Ephesians refers to this mystery now made known as "a plan for the fullness of times, to sum up all things in Christ, both in heaven and on earth" (Eph 1:10).

24. Michael L. Cook, *Trinitarian Christology* (New York: Paulist, 2010), 50.

25. Brendan Byrne argues that both passages rule out any interpretation of pre-existence in a nonpersonal way; see "Christ's Pre-Existence in Pauline Soteriology," *Theological Studies* 58 (1977): 321.

26. Hurtado, *Lord Jesus Christ*, 126.

Thus, the mystery of Christ and the new age that has appeared with his resurrection affects not just human beings but the cosmos itself, made subject to futility but longing to be set free to share in the glorious freedom of the children of God. Creation is groaning in labor pains even now (Rom 8:20-22). Indeed, as Dermot Lane says, eschatology and Christology interact so creatively and continuously in Paul's theology that one cannot be understood without the other.[27] The *eschaton* is seen as already having dawned with the resurrection of Jesus in the gospels, with Matthew's picture of the bodies of the saints being raised and entering the city to appear to many (Matt 27:52). Thirteen times Matthew describes Jesus as the Son of Man coming in judgment. The book of Revelation looks forward to the triumph of Christ over the historical forces, worldly and demonic, that oppress his followers.

John's theology is both incarnational and cosmic. It begins with the great hymn or prologue, drawing on Old Testament wisdom theology; the Word that has become flesh participates in God's creative work: "He was in the beginning with God. All things came to be through him, and without him nothing came to be" (John 1:3). John's eschatology stresses the present while preserving the tension in the preaching of Jesus between present and future. Eternal life is a present reality for those who believe in Jesus; they have received the Holy Spirit (John 20:22), and they will be raised up on the last day (John 3:36; 6:40, 47, 54). They have already passed from death to life (John 5:24, 40). If we are to do justice to the eschatological faith of the early Christians as well as to the biblical tradition, we cannot ignore these passages that speak of Christ's preexistence, role in creation, and future coming in glory.

Metz, with his efforts to reclaim an apocalyptic eschatology, substituting it for a secular, "evolutionary" view of time, recognizes Christ's eschatological role in bringing the fullness of the kingdom. Nor does Tilley deny that the kingdom is God's work; he continually emphasizes this theme.[28] To acknowledge this does not mean that faithful Christians have no role in bringing the kingdom about or witnessing to its presence. Theologians like Schillebeeckx, Metz, Johnson, Nolan, Schüssler Fiorenza, and Tilley are not denying the divine action in bringing about the reign of God; what they emphasize is that the divine agency empowers and works through human beings who in imitation of Christ reach out

27. Dermot A. Lane, *Keeping Hope Alive: Stirrings in Christian Theology* (New York: Paulist, 1996), 107.

28. Tilley, *The Disciples' Jesus*, 31–32, 247–50.

to others in compassionate service or reconciling practices. For example, Tilley maintains that revelation can be understood not just as God's originating, primary act but also as an ongoing, secondary act of God's people empowered by God in, by, and through the indwelling Spirit.[29] For Ellacuría, "[The church's] praxis fundamentally consists in realizing the Kingdom of God in history, in activity that leads to the Kingdom of God being realized in history."[30] As traditional Catholic theology teaches, grace builds on nature.

Church and Mission

Contemporary Catholic theology recognizes a wideness in God's mercy, and it sees dialogue with another religious tradition as a genuinely religious encounter. According to Francis Sullivan, "mainstream" Catholic theology, including theologians such as Karl Rahner, Wolfgang Beinert, Yves Congar, Jacques Dupuis, Johannes Feiner, Piet Fransen, Heinrich Fries, Walter Kasper, Hans Küng, Joseph Ratzinger, Otto Semmelroth, Bernard Sesboüé, Gustave Thils, and Hans Waldenfels, recognizes that both non-Christian religions and transcendent values such as justice, fraternity, solidarity with the poor, peace, and compassion can serve as mediations of grace and salvation for people who do not share Christian faith.[31]

Yet in a globalized world, where the reality of religious pluralism makes dialogue imperative, the temptation is to move from a Christo-centric or even a theocentric theology to one that is regnocentric, putting witnessing to the kingdom at the center of the religious task, as we saw in chapter one. This risks losing sight of what is unique to Christ and to the church. No longer the center of Christian life, the church moves to the periphery. In witnessing to gospel values, Christians join with those from other religious traditions and with other people of good will in working toward the humanization of society. This can be helpful if it brings those who follow different religious paths closer together in working for the common good. But it also risks reducing Christianity to ethics—the perennial temptation of liberal theology. Isn't working for the

---

29. Ibid., 261.

30. Cited by Ashley, "Contemplation in the Action of Justice," 158.

31. Francis A. Sullivan, *Salvation Outside the Church?* (New York: Paulist, 1992), 181.

kingdom sufficient? Do we really need the church? A deficient Christology makes such a reduction much more likely. The Vatican has reacted strongly to these theologies of religious pluralism, as we have seen, insisting in *Dominus Iesus* (2000) that Jesus is the one mediator and only savior (no. 13) and that the kingdom of God cannot be separated from the church (no. 18).

This is not to deny that God's grace works beyond the structures of the church and its sacramental life. The great world religions not only have positive value in the mystery of Divine Providence but are most probably the ordinary way of salvation for their adherents, though the Catholic Church has not gone so far as to officially affirm this. In his encyclical *Redemptoris Missio*, Pope John Paul II acknowledged the Spirit's presence outside of Christianity; he affirmed that the "Spirit's presence and activity affect not only the individuals but also society and history, peoples, cultures and religions" (no. 28), which is to say that the Spirit is mysteriously present in other religions and cultures, even if Jesus remains the one savior of all and so the church must continue to evangelize. Though he did not call these religions mediators of saving grace in their own right, he spoke of "participated forms of mediation of different kinds and degrees," acquiring meaning from Christ, the one mediator between God and humankind (no. 5). Thus Catholicism does not teach that Christianity is the only way to salvation.

Comparative theologians like James Fredericks and Francis Clooney continually warn against the tendency of some religious pluralists to flatten out religious difference by concluding that different religions—for example, Christianity and Buddhism—are really saying the same thing in different words or are different expressions of the same transcendent truth. Fredericks argues that such an approach represents a "domestication of differences," making other religions significantly less interesting because they are no longer really challenging.[32] It dishonors the religious Other by interpreting it in terms of one's own categories. Religions need to be respected in their uniqueness. This includes Christianity. The doctrine of the incarnation cannot be reduced to poetry and is more than

32. James L. Fredericks, *Faith among Faiths: Christian Theology and Non-Christian Religions* (New York: Paulist, 1999), 111–16; for a discussion of the challenges and tensions of inhabiting two different religious communities, see Francis X. Clooney, "Neither Here Nor There: Crossing Boundaries, Becoming Insiders, Remaining Catholic," in *Identity and the Politics of Scholarship in the Study of Religion*, ed., José Cabezón and Sheila Davaney (New York: Routledge, 2004), 99–111.

metaphor; it discloses the truth of the divine self-communication and how we live in light of that mystery, and it looks forward to Christ's coming again in glory to bring about a new heaven and a new earth.

On the one hand, respect for the religious Other does not mean redefining the Christian christological confession in a way contrary to the historic faith or creeds of the church. For example, Paul Knitter sees the resurrection of Jesus as a powerful symbol or myth but not as something true in its historical facticity or in the raising of his physical body. The risen Christ is an expression of the universal presence and power of the divine in all religions. Jesus' uniqueness lies in his preferential identification with the oppressed, rather than in being better than other teachers or Awakeners; like them, he is an incarnation or enfleshment of Ultimate Reality or Ultimate Truth.[33] In cases like this we need to remember Fredericks's warning: "Jettisoning traditional Christian doctrine prior to meeting with other religious believers does not provide a foundation for dialogue. In fact, such an approach guts dialogue of its theological value to a comparative theologian."[34]

On the other hand, in interreligious dialogue or evangelization one does not have to begin with a proclamation of Christ as the unique mediator of salvation. Even if Catholic theology finds saving grace mediated through the incarnation, it recognizes other mediations of grace and sees the divine Spirit of Christ at work in other religions, cultures, and sacred writings. Taking a position against that of Roger Haight, with his "uncentering" of the resurrection, Michael Cook argues that the resurrection is the constitutive cause of salvation for all of creation: "The effectiveness of Jesus' resurrection in the power of the Spirit is available to other religious mediations even though they do not recognize the specifically Christian claims about Jesus."[35] Cook's position is rooted in his fundamentally trinitarian vision.

The dispute between Rome and the Federation of Asian Bishops' Conferences about how to proclaim Christ in an Asian context is instructive.[36]

---

33. Paul F. Knitter, *Without Buddha I Could Not Be a Christian* (Oxford: Oneworld, 2009), 103–126.

34. James L. Fredericks, *Buddhists and Christians: Through Comparative Theology to Solidarity* (Maryknoll, NY: Orbis, 2004), 106.

35. Cook, *Trinitarian Christology*, 7; see Haight, *Jesus Symbol of God* (Maryknoll, NY: Orbis, 1999), 149.

36. See Edmund Chia, "Of Fork and Spoon or Fingers and Chopsticks: Interreligious Dialogue in *Ecclesia in Asia*," in *The Asian Synod: Texts and Commentaries*, ed. Peter C. Phan (Maryknoll, NY: Orbis, 2002), 273–83.

The Asian bishops did not want to begin by proclaiming Christ as the unique savior of Asia, the title of the Roman-drafted *Lineamenta* for the 1987 special assembly for Asia of the Synod of Bishops, though they did not deny it. They did not find this a good starting point in an Asian context. Instead, they wanted to begin with a triple dialogue: with other religions, with culture, and with the poor.[37]

But Phan himself seems to go further. He argues that the mission of the church should not be seen as ecclesiocentric, working to implant the church where it has not yet taken root, but as regnocentric, witnessing to the kingdom of God, spreading gospel values—God's presence in Jesus bringing forgiveness and reconciliation, justice and peace throughout the world, as we have seen.[38] He suggests that the church need not call others to Christ but only to the kingdom of God, "to the way of life and the values that he embodied in his own person, and the 'taking up of his mission' in the service of the kingdom of God."[39] While Phan insists that to proclaim the kingdom of God is to proclaim the Christ event,[40] he seems to separate the Logos and the Spirit from Christ and Christianity: "Jesus mediates God's salvation to humanity in an overt, explicit, and fully visible way, which is now continued in Christianity, whereas other savior figures and religions, insofar as they mediate God's salvation to their followers, do so through the power of the Logos and the Spirit."[41]

But the Spirit cannot be separated from Christ or from the church, the universal sacrament of salvation, as David Coffee maintains.[42] Similarly, Ilia Delio argues against the attempts of some "post-Christians" to develop a spirituality purified of Christ. Such a spirituality of Spirit alone is a denial of the Trinity and hence a denial of Christ. She calls it a spir-

---

37. Thomas C. Fox, *Pentecost in Asia: A New Way of Being Church* (Maryknoll, NY: Orbis, 2002), 158–59.

38. Peter C. Phan, "A New Way of Being Church: Perspectives from Asia," in *Governance, Accountability, and the Future of the Catholic Church*, ed. Francis Oakley and Bruce Russett (New York: Continuum, 2004), 183.

39. Peter C. Phan, *In Our Own Tongues: Perspectives from Asia on Mission and Inculturation* (Maryknoll, NY: Orbis, 2003), 61.

40. Ibid., 38; Phan speaks of the need to combine a "high" Christology with a "low" ecclesiology (31).

41. Peter C. Phan, *Being Religious Interreligiously: Asian Perspectives on Interfaith Dialogue* (Maryknoll, NY: Orbis, 2004), 67.

42. David M. Coffee, "A Trinitarian Response to Issues Raised by Peter Phan," *Theological Studies* 69/4 (2008): 852–74, esp. 872–73.

ituality bereft of any real theology. "To dismiss Christ as the life of the world is to abandon any hope for the world in God."[43]

The mission of the church cannot be described simply as witnessing to or working to bring about God's reign, important as that is. It cannot prescind from the promise that all nations will know God's salvation (Isa 11:9), from Paul's proclamation of the resurrection of the dead, already begun in Christ, and the recapitulation of all things in Christ (1 Cor 15:24-28; cf. Eph 1:10), from the Johannine promise of our share in the life of God as Father, Son, and Spirit (John 14:23-26), or from the promise of a new heaven and a new earth (Rev 21:1; 2 Pet 3:13). In the Christian tradition the kingdom of God is inconceivable apart from Christ, and it is already present in an initial way through his resurrection.

The church itself is an eschatological reality, a pilgrim church journeying through time toward a fulfillment that is at once historical, social, and cosmic, as we have seen. It sees history as moving toward a goal, the fullness of the kingdom that has already been revealed through the resurrection when death will be destroyed and God will be all in all (1 Cor 15:26-28). In the words of *Lumen Gentium,*

> Already the final age of the world is with us (cf. 1 Cor 10:11) and the renewal of the world is irrevocably under way; it is even now anticipated in a certain real way, for the Church on earth is endowed already with a sanctity that is real though imperfect. However, until there be realized new heavens and a new earth in which justice dwells (cf. 2 Pet 3:13) the pilgrim Church, in its sacraments and institutions, which belong to this present age, carries the mark of this world which will pass, and she herself takes her place among the creatures which groan and travail yet and await the revelation of the sons [and daughters] of God (cf. Rom 18:19-22). (LG 48)

Nor can a regnocentric understanding of church satisfy the deep hunger of so many today for an experience of God, for a sense of the holy. There are some lessons to be learned from Latin America, where one frequently hears that the Catholic Church under the influence of liberation theology opted for the poor at the same time that the poor were opting for Pentecostalism. The losses to the church have been enormous. The fascination of some Catholics today with the Tridentine Mass may be a response to what is experienced as a loss of the sacred and the

---

43. Ilia Delio, *Christ in Evolution* (Maryknoll, NY: Orbis, 2008), 136.

transcendent, even if the transcendent cannot be reduced to religious feeling.

The church is more than an experience of community or a place of worship. Nor can it be reduced to some form of the Social Gospel. The church makes the transcendent immanent, bringing the numinous into the midst of the human, disclosing it in symbol and rite, joining time and eternity. The risen Jesus is not just remembered but encountered in a holy communion that incorporates us into his paschal mystery. We have an intimate sharing in his Body and Blood, safeguarded by a tradition that claims continuity with the earliest Christian communities and ultimately with Jesus.

Some Concluding Reflections

1. The eschatological hope of the early Christians found rich expression when they gathered for worship. Their faith was fundamentally communal. They prayed *Maranatha* that the risen Lord might return to bring the fullness of the kingdom, and they faced east in anticipation of his advent. In later centuries this eschatological hope, while never entirely lost, gave way to a much more individualistic understanding of salvation and, particularly in the West, to a fear of the Last Judgment, when "even the just are mercy needing" (*Dies Irae*), while the imagination of the faithful focused much more on Christ's presence in the elements.

2. The Second Vatican Council did much to renew the church's liturgy, with its emphasis on full participation and inculturation, but while it spoke of the earthly liturgy as a foretaste of the heavenly liturgy celebrated in the heavenly Jerusalem (*Sacrosanctum Concilium* 8), it did little to reclaim the eschatological imagination that characterized the early church. Theologians like Karl Rahner, Johann Baptist Metz, Jürgen Moltmann, and Peter Phan have helped recover a richer understanding of eschatology; they stress that it cannot be reduced to an individualistic doctrine of salvation but has a this-worldly, "political" dimension and affects not just individuals and society but the cosmos itself.

3. Because the Eucharist is eschatological in its focus, it is important to give voice to those who are voiceless, the poor and the suffering, the many who have suffered injustice, the marginal, the dead, all those who wait for their ultimate vindication and the fullness of salvation. The es-

chatological imagination places the present under judgment because it imagines a future where justice will have triumphed, wounds have been healed, nature restored, and the dead raised to everlasting life. The transformation of the elements in the Eucharist symbolizes the transformation of all creation.

4. Today some critics, Pope Benedict among them, lament an insufficiently "Godward" dimension in contemporary liturgies that place so much emphasis on celebration, community, and hospitality. At the same time, the substitution of ethics for eschatology, already observed in the early Middle Ages, has been exacerbated in the work of some contemporary theologians by a notion of the kingdom of God that is insufficiently transcendent. If we need to recognize that God works through all who seek the common good of humanity, we also need to stress that it is the risen Jesus who will bring the kingdom in its fullness; his eschatological role cannot be denied.

5. Against the individualistic understanding of salvation so widespread today, with its emphasis on the *eschata*, the last things, we have tried to retrieve a more robust, biblical concept of the *eschaton*. The resurrection of Jesus touches not just our own destiny but that of all creation. A theology of creation implies eschatology because Christ is the source and the goal of all that is, the Alpha and the Omega. We are called not to separateness but to communion with others, with nature, and with God.

6. The resurrection of Jesus means that the *eschaton* has already arrived, at least in an anticipatory form. We must continue to pray for the coming of the kingdom in its fullness. It will mean the victory of justice for all the victims of history, wiping away the tears from their eyes and binding up their wounds. The kingdom will bring reconciliation and peace. The kingdom in its fullness will mean a new heaven and a new earth, for the theology of creation implies an eschatology; it suggests that God will not abandon his creation to the forces of entropy and disintegration, as God did not abandon the broken body of his Son. Finally, the fullness of the kingdom will mean the consummation of all things in Christ.

7. In the penultimate chapter we suggested some ways to bring a greater eschatological focus into our eucharistic celebrations, to a deeper sense of the gathered community as the Body of Christ, and to their own share in his paschal mystery. These include a greater sense on the part

of presiders of entering into the presence of the holy and of attentiveness to the eschatological themes present in the liturgy, a sense that Christ's eucharistic presence is not ordered primarily toward adoration but toward the transformation of the assembly into Christ's body for the world, and some suggestions for a more intentional participation of the assembly in the proclamation of the eucharistic prayer.

8. In this final chapter we stressed that eschatological images and theological intelligibility are not necessarily identical. While we are dependent on images in our understanding, drawing the intelligible from the phantasm as Aquinas taught, the concept cannot be reduced to the image. We can understand much more than we can imagine.

9. In returning to the themes of Christology, church, and mission that have been woven through our narrative, we acknowledged how beneficial the emphasis in christological scholarship on the historical Jesus has been. It has led to a greater understanding of his ministry and his proclamation of the kingdom of God, as well as the inseparability of Christian faith from Christian discipleship. The story of Jesus and his proclamation of the kingdom is as important as the doctrine that interprets it, perhaps even more so. Our interlocutors have argued in various ways that praxis or practice is the key to Christology and is at the heart of Christian faith. Proclaiming the story of Jesus in the context of religious pluralism, the church need not start with doctrine; it begins with his proclamation of the kingdom.

10. At the same time, the church's christological faith cannot be redefined contrary to its historic creeds in the interests of dialogue with other religions, making Jesus simply one among other mediators of God's saving grace and denying him his eschatological role. Such an approach is faithful neither to the Scripture nor to the Christian tradition. It is also less than honest and shows a lack of respect for one's dialogue partners.

11. Nor can the mission of the church be reduced to ethics, to a concern for human betterment, as important as that is. Here a careful theological tension must be maintained. If grace builds on nature, and so human beings play a role in witnessing to the kingdom and indeed help others to experience it, the kingdom still remains God's work.

12. Finally, the eschatological role of Jesus cannot be taken from him. For Jesus is not just a man in whom the Spirit of God dwells; he is more than a model or exemplar, teaching God's special love for the poor. Jesus is God's Word become flesh. The real Jesus is Emmanuel, God with us, who lives in the divine presence and is already bringing the *eschaton* when we celebrate the Eucharist. So like the early Christians, we also pray, *Maranatha*!

Index